SELLING TO
ELON!

Energetic Driver, Likable Communicator,
Obliging Helper, Numbers Thinker

UNDERSTAND, COMMUNICATE AND
SELL TO UNIQUE PERSONALITY TYPES

Mark Holmes

Selling to
ELON!
Understand, Communicate and Sell to
Unique Personality Types

Library of Congress Control Number: 2023912713

Bulk discounts available. For details contact: mark@salesrevenuecoach.com

Publishing Coordinator – Sharon Kizziah-Holmes
Cover Design – Jaycee DeLorenzo

Paperback-Press
an imprint of A & S Publishing
Paperback Press, LLC
Springfield, MO

ISBN -13: 978-1-960499-26-4

DEDICATION

Dedicated to my Obliging Helper and beautiful bride Jeanna, my best friend and still the best proof that I can adapt my behavior to close the sale.

PRAISE FOR MARK HOLMES SALES INSIGHTS AND BOOKS

"I wish every salesperson in my company could read this book."
–Larry Labedz, fmr Delivery Executive, SAP America

"If you're in denial about the way selling has changed, this book is your cold slap in the face. Holmes tells great stories of salespeople who still want to sell the old way." –Chris Lytle, author of The Accidental Salesperson

"Get ready to sell larger, longer and more profitable engagement and services because Mark Holmes unlocks and shares the mystery of how to sell high value products and services in today's economy... simple and highly effective book." –Jim Horan, founder, The One Page Business Plan Company

"Mark's strategies for increasing sales has already produced results... and secured the commitment of two large customers that had previously given us firm Nos!" –Dave Steinmueller, fmr National Sales Manager, Hammons Products Company

"Out of 10 targeted accounts we closed 8 in the first year and added over $11 million in new sales with your process." –Steve Hardwick, fmr Global VP Business Dev., TETRA Technologies

"We've gotten incredible value from Mark's sales process and tailored it to our company to utilize for years to come." –Michael Nesbitt, President, Nesbitt Construction

"Brilliant! He's taken very complex selling concepts and simplified them into a short story that's easy to apply. If you want to win without lowering prices, this is a must-read!" –Sandy Higgins, CEO, The Crackerjack Shack

"After 15 years we still use your service-based sales system. It has

OTHER BOOKS BY HOLMES

The 5 Rules of Megavalue Selling
"I wish every salesperson in my company would read this book. Well done!" -L. Labedz, SAP

The Sales Diamond
"This book is great! It was very practical, real-life insights that can be helpful to any sales organization." -E. McCalpine, Cintas

Wooing Customers Back
"Once I started reading WOOING I couldn't stop. It's everything I've been teaching for years with a lot more umph!" -J. Westrich, Bass Pro Shops

CONTENTS

INTRODUCTION

This is a wonderful time to be in sales. The opportunities to communicate, connect, and convince others of our ideas or products have never been more abundant. In today's marketplace, where customers are overwhelmed with options, it's also crucial to distinguish yourself. And there is now a greater level playing field among professionals and companies.

If you're like most professionals, your goal is to gain every edge possible to excel in your career. That's why this book was inspired by the profound impact understanding the four personality styles can have on your success. Picture this: an insurance executive emailed me last year. He catapulted his career from agent to the owner of multiple agencies using insights from a speech I delivered thirty years ago on personalities. Stories like these from clients and audiences convinced me that this knowledge could benefit thousands of professionals, just like you, to communicate and persuade their customers and colleagues more effectively.

Using an easily remembered acronym, such as ELON, was intentional, and it perfectly describes the four personality styles. Watching an interview with Elon Musk one day was the catalyst to create: Energetic Driver, Likable Communicator, Obliging Helper, and Numbers Thinker. The point is to easily remember the styles and apply the unique characteristics, preferences, and motivators to understand and influence your customers and colleagues.

By mastering the strategies you'll read in *Selling to ELON*, you can tailor your sales approach perfectly, connect effortlessly with others on a new level, and build lasting relationships.

WHAT YOU CAN GAIN

Have you noticed that you occasionally struggle to connect with some customers or coworkers? Maybe the conversation never seems to flow, or you can't seem to move them to the desired outcome. On the other hand, there are those people you create an instant rapport with.

So, why the difference? It all boils down to the unique personality styles that people possess and knowing how to adapt successfully to their preferences for communication, pace, and relationship.

In *Selling to ELON*, we explore the four key personality styles of salespeople and customers, helping you identify, respond, and sell to each with greater skill. By watching their behavior and adapting to meet their style needs, you can transform how you sell and achieve higher levels of success.

WHAT YOU CAN EXPECT

In this book, you will discover the power behind the four personality styles represented by the letters E-L-O-N. By understanding and utilizing these styles to your advantage, you'll be better equipped to tackle three critical hurdles in sales and communication:

1. Building a solid connection and quickly establishing credibility, trust, and rapport.

2. Recognizing the distinct personality styles of your customers and coworkers through their behavior.

3. Adapting your behavior to meet the style needs of each personality type, ensuring more engaging and persuasive interactions and experiencing better results.

In the age of information overload and endless sales pitches, your ability to understand and communicate with various personality types will set you apart from the competition. By reading *Selling to ELON*, you'll unlock the power to forge more effective connections and gain the advantage in every sales conversation.

A VALID APPROACH

Throughout my career, I've discovered that having a valid approach to delivering insights for professionals is the key to successful writing, training or coaching.

Selling to Elon is a culmination of over forty years of research, sales, and marketing experience. It contains valuable insights from seven hundred and fifty data points, including face-to-face joint sales calls with clients in six states, coaching sessions with veteran and newcomer salespeople, personality assessments, and interviews.

Drawing on a wealth of knowledge and expertise, I've studied customer styles during thousands of sales calls and read thousands of articles and hundreds of books on sales, negotiation, psychology, marketing, and leadership. I've also delivered over three thousand presentations and countless coaching sessions for some of America's most successful brands and the nation's best-run small businesses.

My promise to you is that this book's concise style will give you practical guidance backed by real-world results.

YOU CAN FIND EXACTLY WHAT YOU WANT, FAST

The information in *Selling to ELON* is arranged for you to quickly thumb through the pages and get exactly the tips and techniques you want. The book has three parts.

The first part will focus on each selling style's strengths. After you read through this section, you'll have a clearer picture of your personality traits when selling others on your idea or product.

The second part will help you understand each selling style's shortcomings. You'll gain insights into how certain traits might subtract value from your conversations and relationships.

The third part of *Selling to ELON* is about understanding the four main customer styles so you can close more sales. You'll learn ways to identify a customer's personality type in the first few minutes, how to speak their language, relate on their terms, and move them to action.

The Conclusion chapter lists the book's main ideas in a summary form for your quick reference.

An added benefit of using this book's ideas is applying its tips whenever you want to communicate with or convince anyone, such as your coworkers or management.

Are you ready to further strengthen how you communicate so that customers will buy what you sell? I invite you to join me on this journey to uncover the secrets of *Selling to ELON* and transform how you understand, communicate, and sell to unique personalities.

Selling to ELON!

*The author may use the term *product* to include products, services, solutions, and ideas in a collective sense.
*The author's clients' names have been changed whenever appropriate to protect their confidentiality.

PART I

ELON SELLING STYLES' STRENGTHS

1

PERSONALITY POTENTIAL

Over 2,000 years ago, the Greek physician and philosopher Hippocrates proposed a theory identifying four temperament types. These four temperaments, or personalities, are based on observable behavior.

But what exactly is personality? Think of it as an operating system. When you turn on a computer, the operating system performs according to its design and what it's engineered to do. In the same way, we have an operating system called our personality. And just like a computer's operating system, our personality is designed with specific traits and tendencies that influence how we communicate and interact with others.

In fact, our personality style can influence how we complete work and overcome challenges to our goals, making it a crucial area to understand and appreciate our strengths and differences.

EMBRACING DIFFERENT PERSONALITIES

It's essential to remember that personalities come in all types, and no one style is better or worse than another — it's just a matter of perspective. For instance, some folks thrive on risk-taking and are results-driven by nature. Meanwhile, others may prefer a more cautious approach to making decisions. Additionally, some people crave loads of information to make a decision, but there are others who are content with the highlights.

Anyone, regardless of their personality type, can be effective at communicating, persuading, or collaborating with others, provided they can manage their own inclinations while navigating and adapting to those of others.

CAN OUR PERSONALITIES CHANGE?

Most people think their personalities are fixed, but what if you could make minor adjustments that could drastically improve how you express yourself in different situations? It's possible, according to some behavioral researchers and psychiatrists, that creating personas to fit various situations can significantly impact our interactions with others.

Have you ever heard of the expression "fake it till you make it?" Well, it might have some merit. While it's essential to stay true to ourselves, there are times when we need to adjust and be more outgoing, relaxed or careful to make a significant impact.

Dr. Brian Little, an author and speaker, explains that adapting to another person's behavior with our own can be highly effective if the situation or goal we're pursuing is essential to us. And in my experience, adapting well is critical when we strive to build a rapport with a customer.

BORROWED TRAITS

Adjusting to another individual's style can be daunting, yet don't underestimate yourself. Even if it takes extreme concentration, you can bring about positive shifts in your behavior and return to your natural tendencies afterward. Over time, you'll become comfortable using what can be considered as "borrowed traits," even when the situation is challenging.

People have remarkable resilience when they're pushed out of their comfort zones. It's like a rubber band stretching and then snapping back into shape. When people are stretched, they can adapt, learn, and then return to their original tendencies.

Noticing the subtle differences of others and being flexible with your behavior to have a positive impact are both essential parts of using "borrowed traits" when you need them.

UNDERSTANDING YOURSELF AND OTHERS

Mark Twain suggested that grabbing a cat's tail teaches you more about cats than anything else. But is it really the most effective way to learn about these creatures? Maybe not. Before grabbing a cat's tail, it's best to have some basic knowledge of their behavior.

Similarly, selling to different personalities without understanding their tendencies and preferences can be complex and risky. Some customers who are analytical by nature prefer direct and factual information before making a confident decision. However, someone more relationship-driven may appreciate a relaxed pace with plenty of small talk before buying from you. Meanwhile, others may require questions that challenge their views before purchasing.

Knowing your customer's personality style needs and how to adjust to meet their preferences for communication, pace, and interaction, is undeniably helpful in influencing their decision.
And it's vital to appreciate and understand the real you before attempting to cater to people and make them comfortable with you and your product.

WHAT'S YOUR PERSONALITY STYLE?

A typical personality test places people into four types or styles, and most people are a blend of two or more kinds. Understanding these four personalities is essential to creating likability, trust, and receptivity when communicating with and convincing others.

It's an excellent idea to take a trusted, validated personality test if you haven't already or aren't confident in the results of the one you've already done. There are excellent, dependable assessments and there are unreliable, inconsistent assessments. You can find the one I trust when doing my coaching and hiring advisory work with clients. Check the Resources page at the back of the book for more details.

Suppose you haven't taken a personality test before reading this book. In that case, as you read, notice the traits and behaviors that you or people who know you well identify as being some of your strongest traits. Before you finish the book, you'll have a much better idea of your tendencies and behaviors, especially your most noticeable strengths and possible blind spots.

Let's start with understanding the four personalities and their potential strengths in selling.

> **IMPORTANT:** *This book describes the four main styles according to the highest intensity of each.*

2

↗ ENERGETIC DRIVER'S POTENTIAL STRENGTHS

*Determined *Ambitious *Assertive *Impatient

ENERGETIC DRIVER'S STRENGTHS IN SALES
Directive
Dominant
Results-oriented
Takes on challenges
Competitive
Not defeated by loss or rejection
Initiates action

The Energetic Driver possesses a strong sense of self that fuels their behaviors, work ethic, and ability to surmount obstacles. Their confidence and results-oriented nature foster resilience and persistence, enabling them to overcome setbacks and challenges that other sellers might avoid.

They are strong-willed individuals whose self-confidence and communication skills enable significant success in sales. They are highly competitive, goal-driven, and quick to adapt, making them excellent at navigating complex deals and overcoming objections. By maintaining balance in their assertiveness, they can achieve consistent sales growth.

TACKLES DIFFICULT CHALLENGES

It's no secret that I'm an Energetic Driver (with traits of a Numbers Thinker) who thrives on difficult challenges. If you're also an Energetic Driver, you probably know what I'm talking about. Let me tell you a story that explains the nature of this personality style.

Early in my career, I left a Fortune 500 company for what I thought would be an exciting sales position at a small oilfield services company in Oklahoma City. My enthusiasm dwindled when I met Nelson, the veteran salesman in my office. According to Nelson, my 500 assigned accounts were all "loser accounts" with no potential. Nelson knew this because he'd initially been given these accounts and made zero sales in a year. I was frustrated.

Still, being an Energetic Driver, I couldn't walk away or give up until I had tried to prove him wrong — and prove to myself and others that I could be successful. I then mapped out a plan to sell those 500 accounts with the encouragement and support of my incredible wife. My Sales Manager must have known the accounts were losers because he assigned me a $0 sales goal and told me to focus on learning the products. Despite the challenges, I sold millions of dollars in products and services during my first twelve months, becoming the top salesperson nationwide. My boss and Nelson were shocked. When my boss quit a year later, I was offered the National Sales Manager position.

An Energetic Driver derives deep satisfaction from overcoming challenges, and it's one of their most unique traits.

FEARLESS

Energetic Drivers demonstrate an organized, take-charge approach to prospecting. Even if buyers decline to see them, they'll keep trying.

There's an inspiring story of a tenacious salesperson who endured forty rejections over eighteen months to meet with a highly desired customer. After eighteen months of persistence, she landed a prestigious contract worth several million dollars. Fearless.

Several years ago, I was asked to coach a multinational company's sales force on winning sales with high-target prospects. It was fortunate that two of the salespeople were Energetic Drivers, and what they lacked in know-how they made up for in determination. For a reduced fee, I negotiated a bonus if our revenue goal reached at least $5 million in new sales.

In the first year, nearly $12 million in new sales were generated. This included an astonishing closing rate of eighty percent with accounts that had never purchased before or had even granted a meeting. These results were remarkable and rare. Undoubtedly, the two Energetic Drivers' fearlessness contributed significantly to accomplishing the challenge.

INCREDIBLY RESOURCEFUL

The motto of an Energetic Driver might as well be, "If at first you don't succeed, try again, and if you fail again, try better." They want to do it better to get better results faster and nothing will stand in their way if they want it bad enough.

Undaunted by resistance or turn-downs that might discourage or send other salespeople scurrying, Energetic Drivers try something else. Their sharp minds constantly turn, coming up with new and creative ideas that might work better.

One of my fellow salespeople from when I sold oilfield services had a customer that kept turning him down for an appointment. So, he bought a cassette player (1980s technology), recorded a clever message asking for an appointment, and shipped it to the client. A few weeks later, he landed a meeting with the man and eventually a new sale. His customer was humored by the extra effort and couldn't resist the request for an appointment.

Energetic Drivers love a good challenge to put their resource-fulness to work.

SELLS TO ANYONE, AT ANY LEVEL, ANYWHERE

An Energetic Driver will sell to anyone.

Years ago, I read of a salesperson who tried to reach the top decision influencer in a company. Everyone with influence on the decision had already met with her, but the executive repeatedly turned her down. For months, she attempted every angle and every form of communication she knew of to land an appointment with him. She wanted the sale, and nothing short of a padlock would keep her out.

Finally, knowing that a big sale would soon be awarded, she overnighted a shoe to the man's office. Inside the box, a note read: *I have one foot inside your company's door. Would you allow me the opportunity to place the other foot inside your door?* She signed it and included her card. He laughed when he opened the box, read the note, grabbed his phone, and dialed her immediately. After getting her foot inside his door, she successfully won the deal.

STRONG DESIRE TO GET RESULTS

Because they highly value results, Energetic Drivers tend to emphasize how their product or service will make a positive difference in the customer's operations, but back it up with facts and proof. You won't have to tell an Energetic Driver to run the numbers to make a strong case for their value proposition. Their brains naturally think about quantifying value, and they'll not mind spending the time to run the numbers for each customer's situation because they don't want to risk losing the sale.

Driven to achieve results, face challenges head-on and win over any obstacles, the Energetic Driver believes losing is unacceptable.

With an incredible motivation to increase their success, if a challenge to close sales exists, they desire to find a way to solve it and accomplish the goal.

STRONG-WILLED BUT OPEN TO IMPROVE

Everyone called him "Clutch," the top salesperson who resented his boss for hiring me to coach the salesforce. At first, he wasn't thrilled about going through my coaching, especially since I'd tag along as he hunted for new business and called on customers across Oklahoma and Texas.

Nonetheless, Clutch was one of the most determined, skilled, and strong-minded salespeople I've ever met. We traveled hundreds of miles, made numerous joint sales calls, and logged many hours together. Being confined to a car together for extended periods broke down our initial tension and resistance, and we eventually clicked.

Clutch put his tenacious spirit to use and adapted many of my coaching and sales tools, with impressive results. He used breakthrough questions, adjusted his communication skills with different customer personalities, and differentiated his value proposition to fit each buyer. Additionally, he surprised me when he successfully applied my strategic management toolkit to land big accounts.

Don't think Energetic Drivers think they're so perfect that there's no room for getting better, because that's not the case. They're more interested in accomplishing bigger goals faster than losing a little pride over the fact that they could improve personally.

A NOSE FOR THE CLOSE

Continuing with Clutch's story, he might be a bit old school for some (but I don't think so) with his insistence that a salesperson must ask for the business, repeatedly if necessary. But I saw him pull it off flawlessly, and not once did the customer ever react as if Clutch was being too pushy.

"Charlie, I want your business, and I want to supply this product for you," Clutch would say directly, or he'd say, "Now, Charlie, we've met on this several times, I've provided the best solution that will meet your needs, and my price is competitive. I can have this here for you on Friday. All I need is a purchase order from you?"

He was direct, bold, and maybe even a little blunt, but Clutch understood each customer's style and established rapport and respect. And he didn't want to lose a sale for lack of asking.

An Energetic Driver is resolute about going after the sale. If one opportunity didn't pan out, as some of Clutch's didn't, he immediately had another opportunity already mapped out for us to call on. An Energetic Driver will not waste time because, to them, time is money.

THOROUGHLY PREPARED, COMPETENT

This trait is best explained with a vivid story that happened in the IT arena.

A global tech company had hired a sales consultant and trainer to help a high-performance sales team get back on track after sales fell off by fifteen percent. As part of his preparation, he interviewed the sales manager and meticulously combed through the website and any information the company provided. He left no stone unturned.

The training concluded, and the regional VP thanked the consultant and addressed the thirty high performers. He asked the salespeople if they could quote the company's mission statement. Sadly, none raised their hand except the consultant. The VP was disappointed with his team, but impressed with the consultant's preparation efforts.

If you're wondering who the consultant was, it was none other than a competent, thoroughly organized and hard-working Energetic Driver. Their drive for success and competency makes them meticulous in their preparation efforts. They leave no room for doubt or error and invest extra effort in making each customer interaction successful. So, if you're an Energetic Driver, know that your desire to prepare adequately and display your competency speaks volumes to your customers, and they'll trust you to satisfy their needs.

INCREDIBLE PERFORMANCE

Suppose you need something done quickly. Just ask Energetic Driver, because their sense of urgency ignites when they set out to accomplish important goals. They take immediate action, organize their plan, and execute, all with little to no outside motivation.

The Energetic Driver sets high goals for themselves and works with self-determination until they accomplish the goal. Likewise, they can solve sticky account problems without getting mired in drama. Ultimately, getting results is their primary concern.

Steve, an experienced seller working for a client of mine, had an intense Energetic Driver personality characterized by forceful, bold, and overbearing behavior. But he was super bright too, and could back up most of his blunt talk with results and correct answers at the right time. Steve was also the number one salesperson on a team that produced over $100 million annually.

Steve had one of the strongest desires to win I've ever seen. He was direct as a communicator and never held any opinion back from me, regardless of whether he agreed or disagreed. If other salespeople said he couldn't land a particular account, he would prove them wrong.

Sometimes, however, the strong ego of an Energetic Driver combined with what can be an opinionated, impatient tendency will morph into becoming a chronic negativist. That's what happened to Steve, unfortunately. His complaining and grumbling went on far too long, and the VP cut him loose, as painful as it was to let him go.

EXCELLENT PROBLEM SOLVER

Picture this situation: Randall, a new salesperson in New Orleans, took me along on several days of sales calls. His boss hired me to coach Randall since he was still new to the sales profession.

We met a prospect who was inclined towards a competitor to my client. Randall, however, searched for any angle he could use to get past the buyer's resistance. He found a way to connect with the customer and figure out what mattered most to them. We asked about their plans for capital expenditure, and whether or not they were open to an approach that could benefit them. We polished the question until it was suited to the customer's situation specifically, and Randall asked it on the next call. It worked and the buyers responded positively, and Randall's persistence paid off with an initial sale for more than $1 million of new business.

Energetic Driver sellers aren't content to lose a sale until they've tried every possible solution.

3

⚡ Likable Communicator's Potential Strengths

*Expressive *Enthusiastic *Influencer *Cheerful

LIKABLE COMMUNICATOR'S STRENGTHS IN SALES

Friendly
Outgoing
Social
Enthusiastic
Communicative
Optimistic
Persuasive

The Likable Communicator is a personality that radiates enthusiasm and positive energy, which makes them highly effective at getting others excited about their product. Their outgoing and communicative nature also helps them quickly engage with people, building and fostering initial relationships and rapport.

Their ability to focus on the brighter side of things brings a positive vibe to any interaction, which is a plus in the initial relationship and rapport-building phase, thus making their verbal skills a real plus for customers. They are skilled at making great first impressions, and they rarely come up short, unless they get carried away talking too much.

Their enthusiastic approach to selling, combined with their ability to communicate the pros and cons, is appreciated by customers who welcome their solutions-oriented mindset. Most days, the Likable Communicator sells with zeal and can inspire excitement in others regarding a product or service. They have an optimistic and friendly tone that breaks the ice in initial meetings, creating just the right atmosphere to attract people to them.

APPEALS TO A BROAD BASE OF CUSTOMERS

Jonah and Kelly are both successful sales producers with excellent communication skills. They thrive in social situations and use their verbal abilities to connect with people, build rapport, and persuade others. Despite working in different industries and calling on different levels of decision-makers, both handle large accounts and put their exceptional relational skills to work. They have an impressive book of business, where their optimism and ability to inspire customers to take interest in their products produces results.

One of the most impressive things about Jonah and Kelly's sales approach is their ability to adapt to customers' needs and styles. This is what makes them so effective with virtually any type of customer, from Ph.D.-level engineers to trucking company dispatchers.

NATURAL OPTIMISTS

Expressive type sellers love to take on new products and services because it's energizing and fun. They expect the best outcomes and are passionate about their quest to accomplish goals. They're natural sources of optimism for the products they represent.

The talkative nature of the Likable Communicator is on full display in about any setting. They genuinely believe they can talk their way into a sale with anyone in any company.

Kelly is a classic example of someone whose upbeat, enthusiastic approach to selling draws you to them as soon as they walk in the room and greet you. His friendly demeanor reduces customer tension and helps them open up to him more quickly.

MASTERS OF THE ART OF SMALL TALK

As I wrote this section, it came on the heels of a social gathering last evening. We were seated at round tables in small groups, and one man who was newer to the group sat across from me. I noticed at the previous meeting that he was talkative and outgoing. I chuckled when an older gentleman seated next to him said "hello" and exchanged names. Within seconds, the man told everyone at the table his entire history of retiring and moving to the area. He hardly took a breath, and his animated style and excitement to share his background information, which no one had encouraged him to do, pointed me again to the expressive personality's tendencies.

No other personality comes close when it comes to small talk and carrying on a conversation with customers. This strength unquestionably benefits the Likable Communicators' rapport and sales messaging with customers. As long as their communication remains relevant to the customer, small talk will help create a closer relationship and receptivity to their messaging.

COURAGEOUS, CONFIDENT COMMUNICATORS

An international client has an inside salesperson, Wally, who's phenomenal at generating sales with cold prospects. His leanings as a Likable Communicator are perfect in his position, where he has no fear of cold-calling. He will call anyone in any company without hesitation because he loves the opportunity to talk with them and get them on board with his company's products.

To get into a sales career, Wally had to break in. With no sales background, Wally saw my client's ad for an inside sales rep, so he called and asked to speak to the CEO. The receptionist resisted, but was so impressed with his pleasant nature and smooth talk that she buzzed him in to the CEO. The CEO told me how he attempted to turn Wally away and asked him to send his resume in and they'd review it with the other applicants. Still, each time he did, Wally would overcome the resistance and redirect the conversation back to the problem the company was trying to solve by filling the position and how he (Wally) offered the best solution.

By the end of the call, the CEO was so impressed that he offered Wally the job. Six years later, he's still setting sales records. He had zero fear of talking with anyone because his Likable Communicator nature leans toward selling others on himself and consistently getting people to recognize the value of his offer.

ENTHUSIASTIC

A person's enthusiasm is determined mainly by individual choice. Sure, you can learn helpful tips on being enthusiastic, but that will not make any difference if you don't choose daily to live and work with enthusiasm.

I asked one Likable Communicator about the key to her continual sunny disposition. She told me that when she got up in the morning, she immediately went outside to get her newspaper, looked up to the sky, and announced, "This is the day the Lord has made. I will rejoice and be glad in it." Ask them how they do it, and I'll guarantee you they've found a way to reserve ample supplies of enthusiasm and positive feelings to handle the criticisms, rejections, or challenges they face daily.

The enthusiasm of the expressive individual for their product can be infectious, causing customers to take an interest where there wasn't any, and even swing their influence to make a purchase when they're already happy with a present vendor.

In some situations, a customer wants, even needs, to be enthusiastic or excited about what you offer. The Likable

Communicator salesperson can fill that void by turning up their passion for what they sell and how it will benefit the customer's situation.

We can all take a lesson from the Likable Communicator and choose to be enthusiastic.

VOICES THE POWER OF OPTIMISM

The stronger the Likable Communicator nature, the more optimistic they'll be, and it's a good thing because, according to some studies, happy salespeople outsell pessimistic salespeople by around thirty percent. They hold onto incredible optimism in the face of disappointment and rejection.

In a sales profession, optimism is a real advantage. You can have all the skills in selling to make your pathway successful. But, when you're barraged with turndowns to get in the door, or you come close but don't get the sale, you need to be able to reach deep within yourself and find the energy of optimism. If you possess the optimism of a Likable Communicator, you'll stay positive in the face of trials and persevere over obstacles on the way to your goal when others would give up.

DEVELOPS AWESOME CLIENT RELATIONS

It's not often I see someone so talented in a given area that I'd say they've truly mastered that skill. But when I went on several joint sales calls in the field with Arturo, a top-performing salesman in Houston, Texas, I was struck by his incredible social skills. Arturo's Likable Communicator nature became a gift for developing rapport with various customer types. With a high social drive, he was also motivated to seek opportunities to entertain or socialize with clients and prospects at lunch or over drinks after work.

Likable Communicators are natural agents of developing solid relationships and trust with customers, which can lead to remarkable sales results, as Arturo experienced.

HAS GUMPTION

The enthusiastic, optimistic, and people-loving nature of the Likable Communicator could give you the wrong impression. You might presume they're a bit of a pushover and resist rejection so much that they'll cave in to more aggressive customers. At the same time, that can happen. In my experience, however, it's rare.

You shouldn't assume that a Likable Communicator will be namby-pamby when a customer pushes back or is forceful. They have the nerve and the gumption to speak their minds and articulate why they think something's a good or bad idea. If these individuals also have some Energetic Driver behavior in their personality blend, or if they've been coached on how to question and challenge a customer's beliefs, they'll not shy away from holding a challenging discussion.

While they may want to avoid conflict because they're motivated by being admired and accepted, the expressive individual is equally motivated to persuade and win the customer's approval. Thus, they'll use their verbalizing abilities, shrewdness, and creative problem solving to overcome someone's resistance or skepticism.

SMOOTH STYLE

Likable Communicator comes by her persuasiveness naturally, but they also work on it. Their optimism and enthusiasm are evident, especially when they move in and out of conversations as they sell in a room to many people or meet with one person. They genuinely like being around others and being accepted and favored, so being around people is energizing.

To this day, Mike, a retired superstar sales executive and a Likable Communicator, is known in our group of friends as Mr. Smooth. Like many expressive types, he always has the right thing to say in any circumstance, and his comfortable way of starting and maintaining small talk draws you in and makes you want to be around him. He leveraged this ability and enjoyed three highly successful sales careers.

WIN SIZEABLE DEALS

Another Mr. Smooth is my coaching client James, a Likable Communicator who calls on companies in West Texas, where he leverages his enthusiastic personality and ability to build relationships into crushing sales goals and winning sizeable deals for his company. During coaching calls with James, I discovered that his confidence to close deals stemmed from his belief that his verbal abilities could win any account. While that was not always how deals worked out, James worked particularly hard to ask questions and be a good listener. That got him even closer to being an unstoppable selling machine, successfully penetrating and closing large accounts.

4

OBLIGING HELPER'S POTENTIAL STRENGTHS

*Supportive *Patient *Relational *Laid-back

OBLIGING HELPER'S STRENGTHS IN SALES
Amiable
Steady
Hesitant to take risk
Dependable
Compliant
Team player
Good listener
Hides emotions

The Obliging Helper is known for being amiable, patient, and supportive. They take a cautious approach when completing their work, often preferring predictable or traditional outcomes. Even though they may not have the typical qualities of a top-performing salesperson, the Obliging Helper has several advantages over other selling styles.

One of their strengths is being highly adaptable to other peoples' personalities, which allows them to potentially meet various customers' style needs. Their ability to get along with almost anyone gives them an advantage in developing credibility, trust, and rapport more quickly in the sales process.

Customers appreciate working with Obliging Helper salespeople because they're pleasant to work with, and provide excellent customer service before and after the sale, which usually creates a high level of customer loyalty and potential referrals.

STEADY, VERSATILE

One of the critical roles the Obliging Helper provides is that they serve as steady stabilizers, balancing out the extremes of others. Among the styles, they have a more natural capability to put things in perspective and make the necessary adjustments to customers' behavior.

Suppose they deal with an Energetic Driver decision influencer. Perhaps the most challenging style for them to interact with, if they have the necessary knowledge they can still increase the pace, deliver information confidently, ask direct questions, and make sure they emphasize the compelling differences of their offering.

When Obliging Helpers sell to the Likable Communicator customer style, they aren't easily ruffled by their gabbiness and conversation dominance. Instead, they pick through the talk and pinpoint practical questions to guide the discussion and accurately comprehend what the person is trying to say. If they're dealing with the Numbers Thinker temperament, they know not to overpromise or exaggerate anything, and to focus on quantifying the value of their product or idea and asking good questions. They can be incredibly versatile with practice.

Obliging Helpers have the enviable ability to find effective work habits and work consistently regardless of how tedious it gets. As a result, they get the outcomes desired.

TEAM PLAYER

They will do what's asked of them because they're energized by helping and serving others. Since they're stable and steady forces on a team, they're usually well-liked for their easygoing, kind, and low-key personalities.

If you need someone to form a team effort to go after a top prospect, you want them on your team. Their untroubled style and objective logic can reduce a high-pressure meeting to a manageable, pleasant conversation. Their meekness is not a weakness, but it does set them apart from the style that wants to charge their way to a sale when a steady, calculated course would pay better dividends.

The Obliging Helper wants harmony with others. They reinforce for the rest of us that the differences in people shouldn't be a surprise, and they show us how to deal smoothly with each other. They seem to live by the motto, "It doesn't matter," reminding themselves that dealing with others will eventually work out when it gets frustrating.

They're controlled under stress, patient, kind, and as gentle as needed. And yet, they speak their mind freely if you encourage it. But if you cut them off and dismiss their questions or remarks, they can just as quickly clam up, and you won't get their insights for your team.

EASYGOING, STEADY PACE

The Obliging Helper's steady approach to achieve a goal has more in common with the tortoise than the hare.

I've coached numerous Obliging Helpers who are excellent examples of how slow and steady can win the race. Their easygoing, persistent approach eventually results in big goals and top performance. While they might not have a hard-charging pace like some salespeople, their ability to take it more slowly, concentrate on the fundamentals of selling and servicing clients right, allows them to achieve amazing accomplishments.

Francis comes to my mind. Steady, easygoing nature, but could be tenacious when it came to pursuing prospective business and growing sales. She isn't a quitter. And she's not hot one day and cold the next – she's consistent and focused. As a result, my money is on her to finish strong. I've watched her for over twenty years apply what she learns to land big clients!

CREATING LOYAL, LONG-TERM CUSTOMERS

When it comes to creating loyal clients, the Obliging Helper personality is hard-wired for winning people's confidence and repeat business. Let me share a story about Gina, a successful real estate agent.

She'd always been interested in real estate, but felt intimidated by all the misconceptions about being a salesperson. Gina eventually found that her natural Obliging Helper style was far more suited to the industry than she'd thought. And it didn't take long before Gina started making a name for herself.

Her clients were drawn to her patient, easygoing yet competent, professional demeanor, and it soon became apparent that she had an extraordinary gift for creating loyal, long-term client relationships. A reputation for her outstanding service and results led to a flood of referrals and repeat business.

LISTENING EAR

Steve is one of the top financial advisors in one of the top ten-rated banks in the country. In an industry where trust and relationships are paramount, he leverages his calm manner and good listening skills to close more business than anyone else in his company. Steve's boss told me about his success, and I couldn't wait to start working with him.

I was instantly impressed with Steve's Obliging Helper style and how quickly he could set people at ease with his relaxed approach and patient listening.

As your coworker, Obliging Helper will be there to help anytime you need them to listen and to take a sincere interest in you. As a seller, they'll make customers feel liked, respected, and highly valued and reassure them that they understand their needs.

SERVANT-HEART SELLERS

Tim is one of those Obliging Helpers who came to mind when I wrote this book. He works for a client I've served for over thirty-five years, and Tim's a long-term, dependable employee with many skills, including sales. On his personality inventory, Tim has an extremely high "need to serve" motivation, low assertiveness, mid-range score on intensity, and very high personal trust.

With those traits scores, in my experience it meant that my client would likely best use Tim's personality style in solving customer problems and complaints, increasing existing customer sales, and performing customer relations work. In contrast, assigning someone like Tim to a complex sale while trying to unseat an existing competitor in a highly competitive niche wouldn't be a good use of his skills.

Tim did become an outstanding performer at nurturing customer loyalty, solving pesky customer problems, and selling into a niche that required high-touch skills and quick responsiveness. But he struggled anytime he was asked to make a large sale.

The Obliging Helper is a steady, repeat performer, but they need to be in the role that fits their natural motivations.

BUILDS STRONG, LOYAL RELATIONSHIPS

The Obliging Helper is motivated by harmony and peace. So when conflict occurs with a customer, it can be disruptive and stressful because their personal mission is to build long-term customer satisfaction and loyalty.

Obliging Helper Kirk, a commercial loan officer I first coached twenty years ago, has since risen to the top of a large financial institution where he oversees loan production.

When I first met Kirk, he was very concerned that I might try to change him into someone who'd have to be "too pushy." This is often the perception of an Obliging Helper, as it can be for many people when they conjure up images of aggressive salespeople and their minds quickly go to the notoriously pushy car salesman.

Because Kirk's priority was creating positive relationships that lead to sales, he felt the best way to do that was through being a relationship builder, and that's exactly what he did. The consistency paid off, too.

CAMOUFLAGES THEIR EMOTIONS

If you know an Obliging Helper very well, then you understand that their personality possesses strong emotions. What's more, they possess an incredible ability to hide those emotions and feelings.

Being married to an Obliging Helper for over forty years, I know this personality well. However, it's still difficult for me to identify what's wrong with my wife when she remains eerily silent for an extended period. As a result, I eventually know when she's disturbed by something, but I don't know what or who caused it — me, one of her clients, a friend, physical pain, or a family member.

Their camouflage ability affords several advantages in sales. First, they have the emotional stability to keep moving forward after a disappointing lost sale. Secondly, they can compartmentalize their emotions and work steadily toward their goals without showing their deeper feelings. Third, if someone frustrates, irritates, or upsets them emotionally, they can temporarily ignore it and keep working.

METHODICAL APPROACH FOR WINNING MULTIPLE DECISION INFLUENCERS

As a salesperson, Obliging Helper has a built-in practical approach to being methodical. They can manage things efficiently, follow strategy and direction, work patiently with customers and their coworkers, remain calm under pressure, and not insist on something to be their way.

Something an Obliging Helper can do that doesn't always come quickly for others is that they manage multiple influencer relationships well. And you can find them making friends, not just acquaintances or contacts, within a department, team, or across an entire organization.

Partly because they're just so darn amiable, but also because relationships are so important to them personally, they put in the necessary effort to create and maintain ongoing positive relations with multiple decision influencers in a business.

WILL MAKE THE NECESSARY CHANGES

Obliging Helper is motivated by steady results.

To achieve results, they look for predictable systems or processes and may initially resist new methods. Eventually, however, they come around to using what's required, especially if they can see the merit.

Remember, they like consistency, and will respond to making changes with more reluctance and care. Though when they do, don't read that as negativity, but rather as caution. The Obliging Helper individual will make the necessary personal changes for the sake of steady outcomes.

RESPONSIVE

Obliging Helper enjoys serving customers' needs and will go out of their way to make sure buyers are happy with the products or services, and happy with them.

I just finished a conversation with an Obliging Helper type, and she's in the running for a nice size sale with a prospect. At one point in her conversation, the customer mentioned that she was the only salesperson who promptly responded to him with the information he wanted each time he asked for something. Her competitors either hadn't answered or had waited several days. He also mentioned that she was the only seller who brought along one of the company experts so that he could meet them and discuss the installation plan.

A customer can expect the same level of responsiveness from an Obliging Helper before and after winning the sale. They'll ensure the customer gets exactly what was promised, because they know that building positive long-term customer relationships produces repeat sales.

5

NUMBERS THINKER'S POTENTIAL STRENGTHS

*Analytical *Detail-oriented *Perfectionist *Meticulous

NUMBERS THINKER STRENGTHS IN SALES
Attention to details
Quality work
Thinks things through
Accurate, precise
Objective
Organized
High standards

A Numbers Thinker brings a unique perspective to sales. Their thought process is thorough and careful, allowing them to make well-informed decisions for their customers. They prioritize reducing risk in decision-making and action, and thus rely on data and facts to substantiate their claims.

Unlike traditional salespeople who rely on a sales-pitchy approach, Numbers Thinker prefers to use well-organized value propositions that flow logically. With precision and accuracy, they prove the value of their solution to customers. They avoid the use of cheesy presentations and instead rely on the power of data and relevant information to win over their clients.

They make plans and usually have some type of strategy in mind before they pursue prospects, which helps them avoid chasing every shiny rock they see.

A NOSE FOR PROBLEMS

When I'm coaching a Numbers Thinker who has a low interpersonal trust score and a high need to analyze on their personality profile, I know they have a good amount of skepticism. In comparison, someone who's not skeptical enough will trust a buyer's good intentions or promises without sufficient proof, leading to poor time usage or even lost sales.

Numbers Thinkers are what you might call natural investigators, who look for potential challenges. Their skeptical nature helps them spot red flags quickly, and then honestly assess the risks before investing too much time or energy. That's why whenever a Numbers Thinker raises a concern about an account or a deal, it's wise to consider it.

ORGANIZED, PREPARED

Picture this: two salespeople are meeting with a potential client. One walks in disorganized, a few minutes late, and unprepared. Another shows up early with an organized presentation and all the info the buyer needs. You probably know who's the Numbers Thinker, because they're the ones who want things done right and on time.

The analytical-type salesperson is motivated to be well-organized and prepared. To them, a routine or system keeps everything on track and makes sure nothing gets overlooked. Knowing the competition, anticipating the client's needs, and knowing all the features, benefits, and details about the product or service they're selling are all important. They gain confidence and build trusting relationships with the client that way.

INVESTS THE TIME TO BE SUCCESSFUL

Mike is a Numbers Thinker and skilled sales professional who understands that each customer presents unique needs and characteristics.

After a few months of coaching, Mike's effort was impressive and successful. He took the time to think through his sales call goals, anticipated objections each type of customer might voice about his product's value and price, and crafted a clear value message that resonated with customers. Mike also asked thoughtful questions to better understand the customer's needs and objectives.

Mike closed more deals faster than expected by focusing on his buyer's needs, developing tailored approaches for each customer, and delivering clear value messages. This approach proved positive for Mike because it allowed him to truly engage in a thorough conversation about his product with buyers. Customers appreciated Mike's level of detail and preparedness, as it made them feel like their needs were genuinely being considered.

Numbers Thinkers' success may ultimately stem from their conscientiousness to invest the time, thought, and effort required when dealing with each customer's unique needs.

FOCUS ON PROCEDURES, PROCESSES

To Numbers Thinkers, the saying, "Just jump in with both feet and get wet," is counterintuitive. Their nature is to be intentional and thorough and to seek proven means for solving a problem or accomplishing a goal before jumping in without a plan.

Analytical types approach accomplishing tasks with all the necessary information. More than motivated to gather as much relevant information about a customer's issue as possible, they naturally take a question-focused selling approach because they consider the discovery stage a critical step in the sales process.

Any time I coach a Numbers Thinker, they tend to be early adopters of our sales tools, such as the pre-call planning tool, the One Page Sales Call Game Plan, or the FSR Fit tool used to realistically score accounts and prioritize deals for time and resource management. Using good sales tools gives them an advantage over peers who don't.

If you're a Numbers Thinker committed to your success, you aren't likely to "go with the flow" or "shoot from the hip" because you act deliberately and only after you've invested sufficient time and effort in preparation.

MANAGE OPPORTUNITIES BASED ON SOUND DECISIONS

Don, the Numbers Thinker, built a successful pipeline of potential customers. He believed in applying a Numbers Thinker approach to every account and opportunity he pursued. Instead of blindly devoting time and resources to his territory, Don ran our prioritization tool on each customer's potential before deciding how much attention was justified. This allowed him to ensure he only invested enough time into the opportunities that held real promise while not wasting too much energy on those with little chance of success.

His strategy worked wonders as Don managed a book of business significantly more extensive than most could. Each opportunity was researched and assessed before any action was taken, thus eliminating wasted energy and allowing Don to use selling time on the best options.

Numbers Thinkers take a deliberate, thorough approach to managing opportunity.

BUILD RESPECT

Unless they're required to work quickly, analytical professionals will take a slower approach to developing relationships with buyers. As a result, they don't focus as much on relationship building early on as they do on building respect.

To them, respect is created with a thorough, accurate approach to the client's situation and needs. As a result, they like to offer a logical case supported by facts and evidence in order to convince buyers. In their view, building respect creates a bridge to foster strong trust and credibility with their clients.

DETAIL-ORIENTED

Marcus, a Numbers Thinker, was one of the brightest salespeople I've ever met. With a near-photographic memory, he would have all the facts and figures so well formed that if he wanted to, he could easily pick out every potential problem with someone's view and expose their faulty thinking to the point of embarrassment. Most of the time, Marcus used his high detail-orientation and verbalizing skills to close large accounts. In technical or engineering customer accounts, no one was better.

Some people miss the details, but the Numbers Thinker virtually never does. Still, their biggest challenge is learning to read people and adapt communication and social skills to create a comfortable atmosphere to discuss the details that interest the customer, not themselves. They can be very successful when they set aside their preferences and, in their place, consider the customer's unique interests in the details.

PART II

ELON SELLING STYLES' BLIND SPOTS

6

⤳ PERSONALITY BLIND SPOTS

I frequently rent cars on business trips. On one occasion, I sat in the car, adjusted the seat and mirrors, and set off. At first, everything seemed to go well. The car handled well, and I felt comfortable driving it. However, another vehicle appeared out of nowhere when I changed lanes to merge onto the highway. I barely avoided colliding when I slammed on my brakes just in time.

My immediate thought was that a side view mirror must have a blind spot. And that's what it was. At the hotel, I looked at all the mirror vantage points and discovered an important view was obstructed by the car's design. It was right there. How'd I miss it?

A blind spot in a vehicle or a blind spot in your selling can have negative consequences if you're unaware of them.

Part One taught us that each ELON style has its own unique and appealing traits. During Part Two, we'll examine the possible shortcomings of each style by becoming more aware of how our attempts to communicate and convince others can be affected by our blind spots.

We all have blind spots, and it pays to be more aware of them — and how others respond.

BLIND SPOTS CAN CAUSE LOST OPPORTUNITY

Around 400 BC, the Greek physician Hippocrates sought answers to questions dealing with why people reacted differently to similar situations, and why people took different approaches to doing the same things. His observation that we're born with a dominant personality is relevant today, and by knowing ourselves better — strengths and weaknesses — we can adjust faster to situations and find ways to get better results.

Our strengths can help us sell, but if carried to an extreme, they can become weaknesses. This can lead to disappointment and lost opportunities, and any style is susceptible. When I culled through stacks of personality assessments, I identified over forty potential blind spots among the ELON styles. Here is a short recap of what you'll read in the pages to follow.

An Energetic Driver is a self-starter with an intense drive for results, which is essential in sales today. But taken to extremes, they can become too aggressive, impatient, and lose sight of developing relationships.

The Likable Communicator impresses with their ability to communicate, and they also possess an optimistic, upbeat attitude. However, when they take it to extremes, they dominate conversations, focus on themselves and not others, and stray from a meeting's purpose.

The Obliging Helper enjoys people, and their supportive, easygoing nature can be appealing. But if taken to extremes, they lack urgency and are timid in asking challenging questions.

The Numbers Thinker studies the pros and cons of situations thoroughly. Communicating all the relevant facts and figures can give customers the reassurance that the Numbers Thinker knows what they're talking about. However, overloading people with details, something they're known to do, can also overwhelm or frustrate customers.

Just because we don't notice our blind spots doesn't mean they don't exist. It takes courage to acknowledge and learn from them.

7

↗ ENERGETIC DRIVER: POTENTIAL BLIND SPOTS

Jake was your typical salesperson with an Energetic Driver personality. He was known in his company as the guy who could close deals with even the most demanding customers. But he had difficulty seeing his shortcomings.

Jake underestimated the importance of listening to his clients in his pursuit of big sales. He was so focused on making the sale that he forgot to listen and fully comprehend the customers' needs. And that was a big mistake.

Jake's attitude cost him some sales. Customers didn't feel he understood what they needed and wanted because his agenda to make a sale superseded their needs. Salespeople with an Energetic Driver personality tend to dominate conversations and steer them toward their agenda. They may rely too heavily on their own opinions and not take the time to understand their customers' needs. Or they may get frustrated and impatient with not getting results and give up too soon, missing an opportunity for a sale.

Understanding yourself well is critical. If you have Energetic Driver qualities, being aware of how you come across and the reactions it produces in others is valuable. Otherwise, you might be oblivious to how others view you.

SEE NO FAULTS

Energetic Drivers have trouble recognizing they're wrong or need improvement.

Stan, for example, sells industrial equipment leasing services for my US-based client. In the beginning, he didn't want to work through my coaching because he saw no need for improvement. After a couple of sessions, Stan recognized that new tools and insights could further increase his success. It put him on a productive track to accomplish more ambitious goals once he put aside his pride and ego.

Sometimes Energetic Drivers seem like know-it-alls, and that's why having the humility to see one's faults is crucial.

IMPATIENT

By nature, Energetic Drivers are impatient and want results as soon as possible.

If things or people stand in the way of their progress, they don't like it. It is imperative for them to feel like the customer is on board with their approach.

Impatience can also cause Energetic Drivers to sometimes give up too easily and move on to another prospect instead of trying different approaches until they get results. Or impatience can lead them to overlook critical details that could help close the deal.

Moving people to positive action requires patience and understanding. And that's not something Energetic Drivers are necessarily good at.

THE "SEESAW EFFECT"

The "Seesaw Effect" occurs when poor sales results immediately follow great results.

I first noticed the Seesaw Effect in a salesforce while trying to figure out why sales lagged so far behind their goals. It was evident from the small business's performance reports that they neglected to create sufficient future opportunities while concentrating on closing deals in their existing pipeline. A great quarter was followed by two poor quarters as the salesforce closed current deals without prospecting for future opportunities. It was a Seesaw Effect for my client.

The Seesaw Effect is especially prevalent among Energetic Drivers because they're motivated by increasing results faster and spend too much time closing current sales at the expense of prospecting in the future.

FORCEFUL, TOO INTENSE

Energetic Drivers may believe the end justifies the means, but it often backfires.

An Energetic Driver I coach, Angela, sells solutions to manufacturers. In her emails, however, she often capitalized, underlined, italicized, or bolded words. For her, it was imperative the call to action wasn't missed. However, buyers were turned off by her intensity.

A financial planner once tried to get my business, but it backfired. He cold-called me on a regular basis, using a referral from a friend and leaving voicemails that became more direct and impatient. Due to my frequent travel and the fact that I already had a financial advisor, he wasn't a priority for me. Unfortunately, he never considered these possibilities.

Over time, his voicemails became increasingly aggressive. At first, they were slightly cynical, but eventually they expressed frustration. In his final voicemail, he said, "It's obvious you won't call back, Mr. Holmes, or maybe I got it wrong and you're not as good friends with Brett as I thought you were!" His attempt to guilt me into committing to his services was absurd. Forcefulness and intensity like that only alienate potential customers like me.

Too much intensity and not enough tact can backfire on Energetic Drivers.

DISMISSIVE

Like many married couples, my wife and I make a joint decision when buying a new car. A few years ago, we shopped for a car and found ourselves highly irritated by the salesperson's behavior. He ignored the influence of my wife on the decision, focusing exclusively on me.

When the salesman introduced himself, he greeted me immediately but never acknowledged my wife. And during the dialogue, he didn't attempt to include her, but focused totally on me.

As the sale progressed, at one point he said with too little thought, "Well now, Mr. Holmes," no Mrs. Holmes mentioned, "let's write up that deal."

Looking at my wife, I could feel the anger shooting out of her eyes at him, and I said, "I don't think so, bud."

Needless to say, we didn't buy a car from him. Greater than ninety percent of customers leave a business due to bad customer service. We bought a car elsewhere and never returned.

Because they're so focused on closing the sale, the Energetic Driver might not even realize their dismissive behavior.

AWKWARD RELATIONSHIPS

An Energetic Driver is wired to produce results, not build relationships, so they may fail to recognize when a customer wants to build rapport and trust.

When a buyer asks, "How long have you been at the company?" and "What did you do before this position?" an Energetic Driver might miss the opportunity to open up.

Being an Energetic Driver, I remember being awkward in social situations. As a salesperson, I knew I needed to interact with customers and build relationships. Despite practicing interpersonal communication skills, I still felt uncomfortable in some social situations. So, I researched books and articles about interpersonal communication skills, and over time, I adapted much better to situations and my efforts paid off with better sales results. And yet, I know it's something I must continue to improve because my inclinations are results-oriented.

DOMINATING THE CONVERSATION

A regional insurance manager named Alvin once approached me for coaching to grow his business, including getting referrals from existing clients. He agreed to my request to interview a mix of his clients to gain an unbiased perspective and then present my findings and proposal.

During my discussions with Alvin's clients, many complained about his poor listening habits. According to one client, "Alvin interrupts me every time we meet." Another said, "Alvin highjacks the conversation. I once wanted to give him three referral leads, but he interrupted me mid-sentence, so I resisted!"

Alvin didn't like my report findings and tore up our contract, which I was glad to do. Due to his tendency to dominate the conversation and be a poor listener, Alvin missed a significant opportunity to increase sales.

ASSUMES CUSTOMER LOYALTY

Energetic Drivers often overinvest in finding new clients since they assume and expect existing clients to remain loyal. However, as new players enter and others leave, decision influencers in a company may change roles. Therefore, buyers may switch suppliers.

Oilfield sales taught me about assuming customer loyalty. One of my most dependable customers hired a new engineer, and I thought his lack of experience would limit his influence on an upcoming project, but my assumption proved costly.

My two primary contacts continued communicating with me, but I only met the new engineer once. When he took over the project, he awarded it to the competitor of his choice.

Energetic Drivers find and close new business. Still, false assumptions about loyalty can be very costly to the results-driven salesperson who overlooks the possible decision-making changes of current customers as their needs evolve.

THE CURSE OF OVER-CONFIDENCE

Overconfidence can lead Energetic Drivers to overestimate their ability to make sales.

Stephen was an outstanding account manager for one of the leading manufacturing companies in my client's region. Despite his success, Stephen overestimated his sales pipeline. He thought he could win over any decision-maker without fail and would confidently tell his boss, "I know I'll close this sale!" or "I've won over all the decision-makers, and they want to buy from me!"

While Stephen's confidence was admirable, it wasn't always backed up by reality. After working hard to win over a large client, he heard they had decided to use another supplier. Despite believing he could beat any competitor, Stephen lost several sales in a matter of months.

If Energetic Drivers are overconfident, they can overlook essential details and factors, resulting in lost opportunities.

AGGRESSIVENESS

Energetic Drivers may see mixed results from their aggressiveness. On the one hand, they're super productive. But on the other, they may come across as non-relational or even too pushy to potential clients if they don't understand this trait about themselves.

As well as negatively affecting customer loyalty, an aggressiveness blind spot can also affect future opportunities. A results-driven determination can cause them to focus on their goals rather than the customer's needs and insist on making the sale even if the customer lacks interest or the timing is wrong.

Furthermore, they might lack sensitivity in communication skills when resolving customer problems, so they don't listen and respond empathically to customers' inquiries.

WATCH FOR THESE BLIND SPOTS

- **I know I'm right**: Their sentiment is, "If I were doing it wrong, I wouldn't be this successful."
- **Seesaw effect**: Focused on closing sales, not on consistent prospecting.
- **Awkward relationships:** Wired to win sales, not to build relationships.
- **Forceful, aggressive, intense**: Pushing and forcing, not guiding the sales process.
- **Not consistently communicating with customers**: Over-confidence in their ability to retain the customer's loyalty and might not stay in touch sufficiently.
- **Impatience with a lack of results from prospects or customers.**

8

⋀ LIKABLE COMMUNICATOR: POTENTIAL BLIND SPOTS

Likable Communicators excel at communication and relationship building and never run out of enthusiasm. However, these strengths out of balance can become shortcomings.

Last week, I worked with Hal, a new coaching client who has a Likable Communicator style. During our discussions about his personality assessment, Hal highlighted some of his challenges. "I realize now that I get too wordy in sales meetings and my emails," he said. "And I also understand that while I ask buyers pretty good questions during dialogue, I'm not good at creating and planning my questions."

Hal's situation is common among Likable Communicators. They believe they can talk their way into any sales opportunity. While their outgoing personality can often win customers over, it can also cause them to resist planning and thinking through their sales call goals, preparing questions in advance, and considering how to overcome objections – all of which put them at a disadvantage with an Energetic Driver or Numbers Thinker customer.

In their eagerness to connect with others, Likable Communicators may unwittingly monopolize conversations, leading to misunderstandings, missed opportunities, and lost sales. What's more, they tend to spend too much time calling on customers they already know instead of prospecting and reaching out to unfamiliar accounts.

If you are a Likable Communicator, awareness of your blind spots, flexibility, and controlling your strongest tendencies will help you win customers' hearts and pocketbooks.

BIG TALKER WHEN A LITTLE TALK WILL DO

Likable Communicators struggle with harnessing their points, stories, and ideas.

In Louisiana, I was on several joint sales calls with a Likable Communicator. He talked endlessly about his products and services until the customer was bored out of his mind, but the seller didn't notice.

Likable Communicators should focus on the customer, not themselves. A good rule is to spend seventy percent of your time asking questions and listening, and thirty percent discussing the product's capabilities as it applies to your customer's needs. With less than one out of five sales opportunities closing on average across many industries, it's wise to keep this in mind.

EMPHASIZE BENEFITS TOO EARLY, OR TOO OFTEN

After an injury ended his baseball career, Jon pursued a career in sales. He was hired for his first sales position by my client's company.

Jon's worst Likable Communicator habit was overselling. Once he became comfortable with the product line and was confident in his knowledge of it, he couldn't stop emphasizing the product's advantages. Even before the customer's needs were fully understood, he'd deliver another quick pitch about his product.

The rule of thumb for years has been that emphasizing benefits too strongly or too early can cause fifty percent more objections or skepticisms about the product. Because he was so pumped about selling what he knew, Jon spent more time talking about the product's advantages than he spent asking intelligent questions.

It's no wonder his results were disappointing. Customers don't like it when their voice is drowned out by a sales-pitchy-prone seller.

Likable Communicators can't maximize sales until they stop overselling.

OVERTRUSTS

Trusting a customer's purchase promises too much is like trusting cheap pizza under a heat lamp in a convenience store. It might promise to be fresh, but it's still cheap pizza under a heat lamp.

If Likable Communicators put too much trust in a prospective customer's intentions, opportunities seem more promising than they are.

For example, Coach Dave, a business coach in California, asked me to look at what he was doing wrong when he struggled to grow his business. Several potential clients seemed promising, but Dave based his perception of what "appeared promising" on a few positive yet ambiguous client remarks. Because of his zeal, he didn't get the client's needs right and thus couldn't articulate a compelling value proposition. For Dave to see better results, it took improvements in asking the right questions, which helped him more accurately understand client needs and determine whether they fit his skills.

A Likable Communicator needs to balance interpersonal trust with a healthy dose of skepticism.

OVERCONFIDENT

People with expressive, articulate personalities believe they can talk anyone into anything.

Ed, a sales manager for a Fortune 500 supply company, once told me that he had to convince his upper executive boss of an idea. As he began his impressive pitch brimming with enthusiasm, he was confident he could convince his boss. Ed, however, did not consider the executive's style, since he hadn't examined his previous interactions or looked for observable behaviors. Ed's idea was rejected, and the meeting ended.

He'd underestimated his boss's style needs. This was a grave mistake, because he'd assumed (again, a blind spot) that his "outstanding" ideas would motivate his boss.

DISTRACTED BY SELF-TALK

When people are speaking, the Likable Communicator constantly thinks about what to say next.

Jack, an experienced East Coast salesman, confessed to me that he spends more time thinking about his next point than listening and comprehending what his customers are saying. Astonishingly, he would even ask the prospect a question and then interrupt or complete their sentences and thoughts because he had something to add.

Your self-talk can kill a sale because you'll eventually miss something critical, or the customer realizes you aren't really listening and loses confidence in you.

WON'T BALANCE THEIR ACCOUNT MIX

Guide wires help amazing unicyclists ride high above the ground. Wind, however, can affect even the most experienced riders. If the cyclist shifted from one wheel to two or three wheels, they'd have more balance to counteract the forces of wind change.

I talked about Likable Communicator Arturo and his many strengths in Part 1, but his biggest shortcoming wasn't balancing his account mix. As soon as I tried to coach Arturo about improving his account mix, prospecting more, and not relying on current customers to carry him, he flat-out ignored me.

After a few months, his A, B, C, and D accounts still weren't balanced, so I continued to warn him. But Arturo insisted he only needed five A accounts and told me, "Mark, I'm number one in our $130 million division, and I don't need a safety net." He was riding high on one wheel.

The following year, Arturo's sales fell by a massive amount when three of those A accounts cut back purchasing and one was acquired. Without strong accounts to replace them, he fell from first to last in sales revenue and eventually lost his job. By balancing his account mix, Arturo would have protected himself from the sudden, fierce decline in sales.

DISTRACTED, A LACK OF ATTENTIVENESS

The fact that they can also be easily distracted is one of the main reasons why expressive sellers can't focus on critical information. Someone walks by, and they look. They glance at the phone when it rings. When someone gets up, their eyes follow. Because their attention is split, they can't remember names, and they might miss important details.

I've seen Likable Communicators misunderstand the issues that influence their buyer's decisions because they weren't paying close attention, putting them at a severe disadvantage.

In addition to losing sales, missing vital information can be embarrassing if you must ask the customer to repeat what they said because you mentally wandered.

LISTENS WITH HAPPY EARS

There's a term in psychology for the problem of listening with happy ears. It's named the *false consensus effect* because it can cause people to overestimate how much others support their views, ideas, or products. And it can cause significant problems in your pipeline.

Several years ago, when I bought a struggling radio station as an investment, my primary salesman was a Likable Communicator. He was energetic and enthusiastic, assertive, and could talk to anyone. So, I split his time between being on air and utilizing his enthusiasm and social skills for sales.

Soon, however, there was a problem with his sales performance. In almost every case, he'd tell me prospects were planning to place ads soon. He'd say, "The customer said they'd like to do something with us next month," or "They're interested. I just know they'll buy soon."

After two months of continued poor results, I knew I had to act fast. I started making joint calls with him and probed into customer remarks. When he made a call without me, I debriefed it in detail and pressed in on actual versus supposed buyer commitments.

The funny thing is, he couldn't close the sale because he talked too much, didn't ask the right questions, and trusted buyers' promises too much. Since I couldn't commit to coaching him then, I reassigned him to his on-air talent duties, and I worked on closing sales when I wasn't tied up in training or coaching engagements.

Fortunately, sales tripled in less than six months. And it only took improving discovery, the value proposition and adding a few closing questions to make the most difference, like, "Are you ready to attract new customers with the media plan we created together?" Or, "What are the biggest benefits you see from this advertising strategy for your business?"

Likable Communicators must replace racing to a positive conclusion without taking the time to confirm the buyer's commitment.

MISSES THE CLOSING OPPORTUNITY

I was asked to speak to a high-performing sales team for an international IT company. To prepare me for the training, the regional manager shared what had happened during a joint sales call with one of his salespeople. It's a familiar story.

The salesman, eager to complete the sale and with a tendency to be overzealous, was so busy talking that he completely missed the customer's positive buying signals. After continuing for what seemed like an eternity, the sales manager noticed that the customer had begun to lose interest. To help save a potential sale, the sales manager stepped in and suggested that if they received the go-ahead from the customer, they could begin working on his project as soon as next week. The customer agreed, issued a purchase order, and ended the meeting.

The salesman didn't understand his expressive nature's potential shortcomings, and didn't read how the customer responded. He could have lost the sale if it wasn't for the sales manager being attentive to the customer's behavior, and asking for the business.

SELF-SERVING SELLING

Your customers buy for their reasons, not yours.

It's essential to remember that people listen for the reasons that will motivate them to act. Thus, people are motivated to act when you speak their language and discuss their problems and possible solutions. But they're turned off if you use your reasons for why they should make a purchase instead of uncovering and speaking to their decision drivers.

During a two-year effort, the National Sales Manager of a small manufacturer failed to increase sales from one of their biggest customers. In explaining his strategy and messaging to me, it became clear that he'd used self-serving reasons like, "We'd like to meet and talk about our ideas for expanding your products." The appeal focused on him and his products, not the customer's situation. The customer declined his request, of course.

Once he changed the approach and provided compelling reasons tailored to the customer's needs, he landed the meeting and ultimately landed a significant increase in business.

Likable Communicators should honestly assess their value proposition and sales presentation to see if they sound self-serving.

WATCH FOR THESE BLIND SPOTS

- **Takes over a conversation**: "I can talk my way into any sale."
- **Weak at asking the right questions:** Overzealous about selling benefits, fails to accomplish an understanding of the customer's true needs through careful discovery.
- **Listens with happy ears**: "But he told me my quote was looking good."
- **Gets mentally distracted with self-talk, daydreaming:** Misses the customer's pain or gain points, or misses closing signals.
- **Overinvests time:** Prioritizes customers they like or those who like them. Might not follow up adequately with customers they aren't as comfortable being around.
- **Weak at asking questions**: Likes to talk, not ask questions. Might not challenge a customer's opinion with direct questions.

9

⟿ OBLIGING HELPER: POTENTIAL BLIND SPOTS

The other evening, my Obliging Helper wife, who works in sales, watched a video of her coworkers in a team meeting she'd attended. After studying personality styles and salespeople for years, I was still curious as to why. The conversation started like this:

"Why are you watching the video? I thought you attended that meeting," I said.
"I did attend, but I haven't watched the video."
"Did something funny or important happen that you need to watch it?"
"No, I just want to see my teammates on the video."

Watching for those reasons seems pointless to an Energetic Driver like me because it has no perceptible value. In the case of the Obliging Helper, however, it made perfect sense because they're relationship and team oriented.

Obliging Helpers are fun-loving, supportive people who work well with others, which is one of the reasons customers like them so much. However, their strong preference for relational selling and a tendency to resist change and risk often leads to problems with time management, prospecting, and assertiveness. And if they're not careful, they can be too focused on pleasing the customer rather than closing a deal, which leads to missed opportunities and lost sales.

Another common trait of Obliging Helpers is to avoid conflict and confrontation. This can hinder them from negotiating with more assertive individuals like Energetic Drivers. Since they prioritize harmony and minimizing tension in interactions, they might be too quick to give in to customer demands and end up offering concessions that are not in the company's best interest.

Obliging Helpers benefit when they become more aware of their potentially limiting behavior, learn how to make significant changes, and quickly get back on a productive path.

OVER-ESTIMATE THE INFLUENCE OF RELATIONSHIPS ON FUTURE SALES

Obliging Helpers tend to think that past loyalties automatically mean future business.

An Obliging Helper seller called me one day asking for advice. Due to a misread of his relationship with the customer, he lost a big sale. A customer who had previously been satisfied with his products (and him) awarded the sale to a competitor and the salesman was shocked.

A familiar phrase says, "That was then, this is now." Things change constantly, and in my experience Obliging Helper sellers aren't as vigilant as they should be in nailing down future sales opportunities with existing customers.

An Obliging Helper must adapt to a buyer who's more focused on results or the benefits of the purchase than the relationship.

NOT SELLING VALUE

Gregg produced average sales numbers when I initially coached him. He called high-profile customers and had lots of industry knowledge. When I accompanied him on joint sales calls, he seemed well-liked. He exchanged small talk with the customer, joked with them, and enjoyed his job. But Gregg asked only surface questions about their projects and needs, and he didn't move the sale forward.

Obliging Helpers work hard to build relationships and trust with their customers, but they also need to learn how to close more effectively and sell value. They tend to sell value by using the buyer-seller relationship. When you're dealing with a buyer whose only concern is the value of the product, that doesn't cut it.

During one sales call, Gregg said, "Mark, I realize I don't do as well with a bottom-line customer."

Gregg's not alone because many Obliging Helper types find it challenging to differentiate and sell high value to assertive or analytical buyers.

DOES NOT PENETRATE AN ACCOUNT ADEQUATELY

A popular trait of Obliging Helpers is their easygoing nature. But it can also be a primary cause of failing to influence enough decision-makers in an account.

One CEO/Sales Manager discovered that his veteran salesperson had only established two contacts with one of their biggest customers. I advised him to investigate further, and he found several more accounts at similar risk. He explained his concern to me in a phone call one afternoon. I told him, "You should be alarmed... your company is probably losing sales you never even hear about or get the chance to bid on."

Obliging Helper sellers have a bad habit of no longer expanding their influence after establishing positive connections with one or two people in an account. To ensure thorough coverage and maximize the sales potential, they must win the support of all the account's decision influencers.

UNMOTIVATED TO CHANGE

It can be annoying to coach someone who appears willing to make improvements but later resists. Obliging Helper individuals can be unmotivated to make personal changes.

Obliging Helper Nate assured his boss and me that he would apply the learning and work on any necessary improvements, but his commitment fizzled only a few weeks later. I have a no-nonsense approach to coaching, so I confronted him about it.

Nate was stunned that I'd confronted him. But once we talked it through and he could see that I was serious, he apologized, explained what was going on, and signed a contract with me to make the necessary changes.

If an Obliging Helper personality lacks the urgency to change, they'll benefit from accountability and encouragement.

LACK OF PRIORITIZATION

Many Obliging Helpers score high on the "need to serve" scale on their personality assessment.

Positive aspects include their service-mindedness, pleasant attitude, and people-loving nature. Negatives might consist of time management, prioritizing, and organizing sales efforts. Here's an example.

Christina was an energetic, capable salesperson with a kind and pleasant personality. She was always willing to help, whether it was a teammate or a customer. Despite her sincere intentions, she often neglected other aspects of her job, like prospecting for new customers and regularly connecting to existing ones.

When Obliging Helpers don't prioritize their opportunities effectively, they almost always don't reach their goals. Rather than finding new business and keeping up with all their existing customers, they cater to the needs of a few preferred customers.

At least once a week, Obliging Helpers should get organized, prioritize their opportunities, make actionable lists, set deadlines, and stop overserving some customers and coworkers at the expense of effectively serving and selling everyone else.

TIME WASTERS

The Vice President of a client's company asked me to help her team manage their time better. At first, she didn't realize how much time she wasted putting out fires, not organizing herself better, and wasting too much time on low-priority tasks.

It's a problem for everyone though, not just Obliging Helper sellers. Our company's training, coaching, and books teach salespeople how to identify their time wasters and get at least eighty hours of new selling time each year.

The types of time wasters Obliging Helper types tend to experience include over-servicing existing business, procrastinating on prospecting, poor organization, and unnecessarily extending conversations with coworkers or customers. On our break at a training conference, an insurance sales manager admitted to me that he'd identified enough time wasters to save over four hundred hours a year — time that he could now invest in closing more deals.

An Obliging Helper's laid-back, relaxed style of accomplishing goals is rife with opportunity to waste valuable selling time. They can have more success by eliminating time wasters.

LACKS SUFFICIENT SKEPTICISM

Tom, an Obliging Helper, believes buyers will be honest about their decision-making role in the purchase. When people are Obliging Helpers, they often have a low level of skepticism and thus accept what people tell them.

In Tom's case, his high trust led him to waste nearly fourteen months contacting the wrong person. He trusted the decision influencer's assertion that he was the sole decision-maker for a big project. When Tom attempted to close the deal, he discovered that someone else was making the final call, someone he hadn't contacted often enough.

His lack of objectivity cost him the sale plus a startling amount of lost opportunity selling time. Rather than accepting the decision influencer's claim, the Obliging Helper seller must balance trust with sufficient skepticism.

STRUGGLES WHEN THE RELATIONSHIP ISN'T PRIORITIZED

One of my most knowledgeable coaching clients is Stuart, who works at the US division of a European manufacturer. His biggest challenge is when customers ignore the relationship. So, when customers don't appreciate his attempts to build a connection, such as engaging in small talk to create rapport, he forces himself not to feel snubbed.

The rejection Stuart and other Obliging Helpers may experience isn't always deliberate. When decision-makers primarily focus on the results, relationships are often a low priority.

Stuart's knowledge of styles and the ability to adapt now allows him to modify his preferences for relationships to make even non-relational buyers comfortable buying from him.

JUGGLING TOO MANY BALLS IN THE AIR

Obliging Helpers definitely want to finish what they begin. Completion gives them fulfillment and the reassurance that they'll return to a regular routine. They do better when they have a manageable number of accounts and know which ones to prioritize.

The Energetic Driver, on the other hand, thrives on managing multiple projects or deals at once. Obliging Helper salespeople can find it exhausting to keep much sales activity going simultaneously.

The most significant risk from an Obliging Helper attempting to juggle too many accounts or selling activities at once is that they'll let some opportunities slip through the cracks.

AVOIDS CONFRONTATION

One of the sellers I coached told me how she avoided upsetting a customer on a contract. I asked her why she didn't challenge the customer's wishes, since not doing so could disadvantage him in the long run. This is what she said: "My goal was to prevent conflict and avoid damaging the goodwill I've built over time."

I warned her against doing that. "What if, for example," I asked, "the customer sees the potential disadvantage and wonders why you didn't advise him otherwise?" She got it, contacted her customer, and discussed the potential risks. Her customer expressed appreciation for bringing up that risk because their team had just discussed it.

Rather than discuss differences of opinion with the customer, the Obliging Helper's nature is to avoid confrontation.

NOT HANDLING SALES FRICTION EFFECTIVELY

Avoiding any and all friction can lose sales and create customer dissatisfaction. Without the right amount of assertiveness from the seller, a buyer might not rethink their situation or make the necessary changes to buy the product. Three potential situations can result from this.

First, they might feel you're not taking their business seriously enough. Second, they could believe you don't fully understand and can handle their needs. Third, they might conclude that you don't bring enough value to their decision-making because you aren't asking tough questions or bringing problems to their attention. Any of these situations can create the potential for a loss of sales.

It's difficult for Obliging Helpers to walk a tightrope with some customers. Too much pressure leads to frustration, and with not enough pressure, they don't buy.

The bottom line is that winning challenging sales requires assertiveness, a sense of urgency, and a drive to close the deal. Savvy customers realize this, and they expect a salesperson to ask questions that make them think and challenge viewpoints that aren't accurate.

UNDERESTIMATE AGGRESSIVE BUYERS' NEEDS

Imagine two people meeting for the first time. The Obliging Helper is friendly and engaging, taking the time to get to know the other person before jumping into a serious conversation. The aggressive buyer wants to dive right into the discussion about the product, his operational problems and concerns, and doesn't really care to get to know the salesperson.

That scenario shows how Obliging Helper sellers must adjust to working with less socially inclined buyers.

Since the Obliging Helper has a laid-back, cautious yet steady pace, they'll likely seek to get to know the customer first before presenting in-depth details about the product or service. The aggressive buyers, however, want to understand the information and to know what results they can expect. They won't invest much time in social interaction or building relationships until they feel you and your company are credible and trustworthy.

Creating harmony in conversations is essential, but Obliging Helper sellers must also meet the expectations of information and be prepared to guide the meeting at a faster pace more to the liking of an energetic, results-oriented buyer.

OVERSELLS CAUTION

At times, an Obliging Helper seller will overstate risks and potential concerns to buyers. As a result, customers might be scared off and turn to competitors.

For instance, an Obliging Helper came to me after losing two significant opportunities. Both customers said she didn't distinguish her solution's benefits from the competition and didn't come across as confident in her recommendations.

Looking back, she could see that the caution she had expressed to the customer regarding the planned implementation overshadowed the value of her product's reliable track record. Although she built positive relationships with her customers and looked out for their long-term interests, she also had to demonstrate sufficient confidence, have a mindset for closing the sale, and focus on how her product would achieve the customer's desired results.

Obliging Helpers must balance caution with an emphasis on the product's value.

WATCH FOR THESE BLIND SPOTS

- **Will not risk rapport with customers or prospects by challenging viewpoints.**
- **Tested by the customer that doesn't prioritize the relationship, just wants the bottom-line.**
- **Misses opportunities to close with some buyers**: Passive, cautious, laid-back style.
- **High need to serve:** Being helpers at heart, they prioritize servicing existing customers and neglect allocating sufficient time for prospecting or closing deals.
- **Slow to sense changing customer preferences:** Relies on past loyalties for future sales.
- **Lacks a sense of urgency, especially if discouraged or lacking confidence.**

10

～ NUMBERS THINKER: POTENTIAL BLIND SPOTS

Dusty had been on the phone covering details of the project with his client's two decision-makers for a long while. Finally, as he said, "Goodbye," one of them thought Dusty had hung up already and said, "Geez, that was long!" The other person agreed, "I know. His stories wore me out."

Little did they know that their comments hadn't gone unheard. Dusty quietly hung up, embarrassed. And Dusty, well, that was actually me. Maybe it's you, too, if you have strong analytical tendencies and the desire to be precise. Overloading people with details and lengthy stories or examples packed with information, however, can work against your efforts to persuade others.

A salesperson with an analytical personality tends to obsess over details and numbers. Over-analyzing data can lead them to spend too much time scrutinizing details with customers without making sufficient progress toward closing the sale. And an intense analytical approach can come across as being aloof and distant when building rapport and establishing trust with clients is crucial.

Analytical types live by the phrase "details matter," which is a strength when it's under control but a weakness when the customer prefers "less is more."

TROUBLE WITH SMALL TALK

Small talk is difficult for analytical sellers because they overanalyze what people say and what to say in response.

My friend Alan, who owns a wedding services business, struggles with small talk at events where he meets potential clients. He once said to me, "When someone comes by my open house booth tonight, I'll say, 'Hi, I'm Alan.'" I asked him what he'd say after that, and he said, "That's the problem. I don't know where to go from there."

His brain goes into lockdown. Being conversational is stressful for him. Salespeople with analytical leanings can have poor social skills and feel awkward at handling informal communications.

INFLEXIBLE, OVERSENSITIVE

The phrase "In God we trust, all others use facts" describes the strong Numbers Thinker. Because they seek proof, data, and many facts to support their claims, they believe others do as well.

In a coaching session, Numbers Thinker Mike mentioned that he felt his entire presentation had failed when a customer objected to his information. When asked how he handled it, he said, "I found it challenging to regroup my thoughts and be more flexible. Concentrating on my customers' needs wasn't where my thoughts naturally flowed."

Another seller is Cheryl. She's a Numbers Thinker who presents information systematically but then stresses if a buyer questions her because she feels it defies her knowledge.

Cheryl and Mike would be better off considering a buyer's questions as possible interest or clarification of something they want to understand, and not assuming the buyer is rejecting them.

LACK OF PREPARATION FOR DIFFERENT CUSTOMER STYLES

The analytical salesperson prepares well for the informational part of the sales call but might not prepare themselves for the people factor.

When I held a training session in Houston, a bright Numbers Thinker named Travis said, "I get thrown off when a customer says something I'm unprepared for." When I asked how much time he'd spent preparing to deal with different customers, different communication preferences, etc., a blank look crossed his face.

In spite of his bright and capable sales skills, Travis wasn't spending enough time preparing for his customer interactions. Different communication styles and preferences for rapport and trust building often caught him off guard.

On one particular sales call, it became apparent that his customer's communication style differed significantly from what Travis was expecting. They wanted him to relate well, listen closely, and have conversations focused on thought-provoking questions. Unfortunately, Travis wasn't ready for this and instead plowed through the data and numbers he thought were critical for the buyer to understand.

When the customer asked Travis about other customer experiences with the product, he responded with a detailed report of their product features and benefits instead of having a simple conversation like the customer wanted. Travis requested a follow-up meeting, but it wasn't granted.

A Numbers Thinker doesn't just need to be smart and detail-oriented, he or she also needs to understand behaviors and to prepare sufficiently for different types of customers.

YIELDS CONTROL TO AVOID CONFLICT

Numbers Thinkers prefer to avoid risk and conflict, which may cause them to surrender control of the dialogue prematurely.

One highly successful seller, Aundrea, described how she used to surrender control to her customers to avoid disagreement. "Once, I had a customer who wanted to emphasize exactly how he wanted the contract to read, so I did what he wanted. But some difficulties surfaced, and a third party questioned why it was written that way," she said. "He agreed when I reminded him that the language was his and that he'd insisted on using it, but I could tell he was displeased that I didn't push back with an explanation of my concerns."

The best solution for a buyer sometimes means challenging their viewpoints. It builds trust and creates a positive impression by making customers feel like their needs come first.

THEY WASTE CUSTOMER TIME

There are two major complaints from B2B decision-makers: "My salesperson wastes my time," and, "My salesperson doesn't add value." Why do they say that? Because it's true.

The age-old saying "people buy from people" is still valid. Numbers Thinkers bring advantages to the conversation, such as the ability to look at all sides of a problem, identify the root cause, and make data-driven decisions. They also tend to be more organized, detail-oriented, and logical in their thinking.

You might think that with those skills, they'd be naturally gifted at persuasion and articulating a compelling value proposition. But I've found nearly the opposite is true. They can get so bogged down in the analysis, details, and data that they underperform at presenting the most compelling benefits and linking their solution's value to the customer's drivers.

Numbers Thinkers prefer to communicate every piece of data they think will make a difference in the customer's decision. Deals are killed by too much information, not developing a game plan for meetings, and not asking enough of the right questions.

Consequently, buyers can quickly be on "overload" by a Numbers Thinker's messaging and feel like the seller isn't relevant enough to their situation.

WHAT'S EMOTION GOT TO DO WITH IT?

You might have heard the expression, "Logic makes a buyer think, but emotion makes them act." Essentially, we buy on emotion and justify with logic.

Your customer's logic or reasons for buying are critical, but so is the emotion behind the decision. The first time I attempted to explain to a Numbers Thinker how buyers use their feelings and rational thinking, the individual couldn't grasp it. Although she was a brilliant, articulate salesperson, she didn't understand how emotions influenced customer decisions. "Purchasing our product is a technical decision," she told me, "and feelings have no bearing."

Analytical sellers often feel this way, primarily if they sell specialized, complex products or services and don't realize that people use logic *and* emotion when making significant decisions. But technical buyers do feel and use emotions, just like their non-technical counterparts.

Even highly emotional people use rational reasoning when deciding, and even the most logical person is influenced by emotional factors. Doesn't it make sense then to appeal to someone's emotional side of the decision, too? Plus, doesn't an overemphasis on facts and figures and data with buyers risk their decisions ending up in a heap of paralysis of analysis?

Here's something a CEO said to me during our first meeting to discuss his company's needs: "Our customer service sucks and it's killing sales!" Can't you picture his disappointment and anger? The CEO's rational mind said something had to be done to improve sales, and his anger (emotion) about the company's poor service hit a fever pitch and he was ready to take action.

The Numbers Thinker must remember that appealing mainly to the buyer's logic will miss recognizing the feelings driving the decision.

MISS THE SUBTLE CUES OF VALUING RELATIONSHIP BUILDING

Analytical sellers tend to be introverted and task-oriented rather than people-oriented. And they might miss subtle signs of relationship-building that their customers value.

Several years ago, I made an error when I assumed that my prior experience working with the company's president would give me an edge. In the first few minutes of meeting with him and his HR Director, they tried to build a relationship and comfort with me. Still, I didn't catch their signals because I was too focused on analyzing and understanding the need that prompted their call. Before I knew it, I'd unwittingly imposed my selling style preferences on him and his HR director.

Because I didn't make them comfortable with me, the HR director wasn't sure I could make the relationship connection and coaching she wanted for her team. So she hired someone else.

Sharing this story with you is humbling, if not embarrassing. If you have Numbers Thinker or Energetic Driver tendencies, understand how easy it is to miss subtle signs of interest in creating trust and rapport before getting into the business issue or problem.

AVOIDS PROSPECTING AND COLD CALLING

Fritz sells for my client, and he's a Numbers Thinker with good verbal skills. When I discussed his personality assessment results and what could potentially be challenging in his ongoing business development, he reassured me that he was talented at prospecting and cold-calling. Despite his confidence, I advised Fritz's sales manager to keep close tabs, since the assessment pointed out possible blind spots regarding the type of prospecting he was expected to do.

After six months, the manager was very dissatisfied with his sales. According to his call activity, Fritz mainly prioritized his time for taking care of existing customers and he had avoided prospecting almost entirely.

Suppose an individual has low drive intensity and low assertiveness scores in their personality test. In that case, they are more likely to seek comfort in selling activities with existing customers and lack the confidence to cold call since positive outcomes are not guaranteed. This tendency becomes particularly strong among the highest-intensity Numbers Thinkers.

AVOIDING CLOSING

Over the years, many Numbers Thinkers have come through my coaching and offered a variety of excuses for not trying to close a sale.

One example is a salesperson named Luke. He and I have been on several joint sales calls together. After a positive call where the buyer had a present need and showed genuine interest, I asked him why he didn't close. As he put it, "I was waiting for him to show more buying signals."

The analytical seller has a bad habit of over-analyzing everything. If they believe they've done enough to persuade the buyer, they'll wait for obvious signals of buyer interest. They might make excuses like, "I was waiting for the customer to take some initiative," or "He seemed like he was in a bad mood, and I didn't think it was a good time to close." The problem is that by waiting for the 'perfect time' to close, they miss out on potential sales opportunities.

A second problem for them is that if they feel uneasy with people, they may lack confidence in closing deals, either avoiding them or appearing unsure when they try. A third closing problem is they can get stuck endlessly gathering information instead of closing the deal. Their need for precision and details to feel comfortable overrides their attempts to close the sale.

MISSING A CRITICAL VALUE DRIVER

After a sales call with Phil, who sells for my client, he wanted to know what I thought. "First of all," I said, "how'd you feel about the buyer's subtle emphasis on safety?" I thought he'd heard it too, but Phil countered, "I didn't hear him speak about safety."

After I mentioned two instances where his customer had briefly mentioned safety, Phil admitted he'd missed it completely. As a teachable moment, I asked Phil, "Were you thinking about the technical data you wanted to present?" Phi said, "Yeah, I have certain information that I think all customers should know about our products, and I didn't want to leave without telling him everything."

Turned out that the issue of safety was very critical to future sales with Phil's client. The analytical seller can miss subtle messages from the buyer when they focus more on presenting everything they think is important to cover rather than understanding what the customer is actually saying.

WATCH FOR THESE BLIND SPOTS

- **Paralysis of analysis**. Spends too much time analyzing and tends to do an info avalanche.
- **Resists prospecting:** The stronger this trait is present, the more the salesperson seeks comfortable sales activities; may lack the confidence to cold call.
- **Misses the significance of emotion in the decision**. Appeals to logic and reason with facts and figures. Misses the opportunities to sell to emotion.
- **Warms up slowly to new prospects**: Questions may be blunt, using formal dialogue. Misjudges the value of developing rapport and receptivity in the early stages.
- **Emphasizes the functional, technical appeal of the product.** Misses the benefits the customer finds attractive.
- **Avoids closing**: Waits for obvious signs to close; endlessly collects information to feel comfortable and wants precision in their preparation before closing.

PART III

Selling to ELON Customer Styles

11

Meeting Customer Styles' Needs

If you've been through any old-fashioned sales training at some point in your career, someone might have told you to follow the first three letters of the alphabet, ABC, which stands for "always be closing." The salesperson must never give up, but push until the customer says "yes" and signs the contract.

Always be closing. Initially, it was beneficial because it kept salespeople focused on winning deals. Yet buyers today don't appreciate being pitched to by someone who doesn't take the time to understand their needs, or someone who gives the same spiel to them they do to everyone.

Some of the best advice I've gathered from my ongoing research on selling to different personalities comes from ancient wisdom. The Roman orator Cicero wrote, "If you wish to persuade me, you must think my thoughts, feel my feelings, and speak my words."

In other words, to be successful, you must understand each customer's personality style needs. Refrain from lumping customers into tidy groups. And don't use preconceived beliefs such as "I already know what they need."

Selling anything today involves seeing the world through another person's eyes and getting their perspective. By doing this, it's much easier to adapt to their preferences, communicate effectively, and make them feel heard and understood.

KNOW HOW TO ADAPT

You might be familiar with the movie *Finding Forester*. The older man and reclusive Pulitzer Prize-winning author, played by Sean Connery, said, "We fear what we don't understand. When we don't understand, we form our own perceptions."

You never want to rely entirely on your perceptions or experience to adapt to a customer's personality style. We might be able to identify the customer's personality type accurately five, six, or even seven out of ten times, but knowing how to adapt and meet someone's style needs is a very different matter. For instance, you need to know how to create communication, trust, and rapport for people to see that your offer has merit, and to buy into you as a person, how you sell, and your product.

ADAPTING FASTER WITH A PROVEN METHOD

Adapting our behavior to be flexible with others can be challenging. One of the best ways I've found that sees positive results is through self-directed activities.

For example, let's say you realize you tend to be talkative and need to be briefer and to the point. To be less talkative, use this activity: practice attentive listening and talking less with coworkers or with family. Replace wordiness with asking more questions, and restate what others say for clarification. Don't draw attention to your viewpoint so quickly. Focus on others.

Or, if you're uncomfortable with small talk and clam up and don't know what to say after introducing yourself, try this activity: write out ten conversation starters and ten questions to generate discussion with others. Put them on index cards, draw several randomly, and practice the techniques before a meeting.

Applying self-directed practices that target your biggest challenges will lead to making positive changes faster, and help you engage customers in ways they like.

In Part Three, you'll learn how to quickly identify the customer's style so you can adjust your interaction to meet their needs.

12

⚡ UNDERSTAND THE
ENERGETIC DRIVER CUSTOMER

People with Energetic Driver personalities usually seem confident, outspoken, and direct in the first several minutes of meeting them. They initiate a conversation with an assertive attitude, make intense eye contact, and have a powerful presence. Their body language and how they respond to questions can reflect how quickly they can make decisions.

When it comes to small talk, Energetic Drivers often take charge of conversations and steer them in their desired direction. They ask questions and expect competent responses from others. They prefer shorter conversations rather than long-winded ones and may become impatient if conversations linger too long.

Instead of ambiguity or subtlety, they express themselves with certainty. They use blunt and frank language, preferring honesty and clarity over politeness and ambiguity. Rather than ramble on hesitantly, they'll explain themselves confidently and complete their thoughts.

Interaction-wise, Energetic Drivers may come across as intimidating due to their high energy, decisiveness, and strong presence. Even so, once they've established a comfort level with another person, they can usually be open-minded listeners.

How to Spot an Energetic Driver in 4 Minutes:

- Greets with formality, direct eye contact, a firm handshake.
- Outspoken, to the point, opinionated, assertive.
- Decisive, fast-paced.
- May direct the discussion, interrupt, correct or challenge.
- Bottom line, results-driven, focused on tasks not people.
- Risk taker if better, faster results are possible.

Additional Behavior to Watch:

- More skeptical than trusting; challenges opinions and ideas.
- Communications, whether verbal or written, are concise. Uses bullet points.
- States their opinions as facts.
- Capable of making quick decisions or conclusions.
- Emphasizes tasks and efficiency; can be impatient.
- Uninterested in your personal problems, indifferent to small talk.
- Email/texting: direct, straightforward with little explanation; to the point; uses assertive words or tone; may be forceful, demanding; focused on results and goals.

ADAPT TO THE ENERGETIC DRIVER CUSTOMER

Think about how your style might best adapt to the Energetic Driver's style.

If You're an Energetic Driver: Because you know their basic tendencies, communicating and relating to them will be easier. You're both competitive, direct, and unafraid of conflict. As long as your style makes them feel comfortable, they'll not mind being guided through your sales process. Don't overload your presentation with information. Keep it short and sweet and hammer away at results or desired outcomes.

If You're a Likable Communicator: You're motivated to get to know them and for them to get to know you. However, you should avoid attempting to build personal relationships too quickly.

Unlike you, they won't enjoy prolonged chit-chat and personal conversation. They think logically, so don't present information critical to your value proposition without evidence and facts. Allow them to lead the conversation if they wish, and pull back from talking too much. Use questions to guide the conversation. Don't feel obligated to agree with everything they say or think. Don't be put off by their strong opinions and ideas.

If you're an Obliging Helper: A harmonious relationship is something you'll strive for. An Energetic Driver will be skeptical, so be direct and emphasize logical ways your product can improve performance. Ask questions, challenge their views when necessary, and talk less. They usually like a faster pace, so they move through information more quickly. Don't be intimidated by their brash and direct tendencies. They value competence and confidence and want to understand the outcomes you can deliver.

If you're a Numbers Thinker: Data is critical to them, but don't overdo it since they need much less than you. Ask questions to uncover obvious, underprioritized and unrealized needs. From what you learn in discovery, make a direct connection to your product's benefits. Acknowledge their opinions or insights — genuine compliments build rapport faster than small talk. They'll appreciate a clear focus on the results they can expect and the difference your product will make in their situation. Because they can make quick decisions, you shouldn't be surprised if they buy your product or service faster than you think is logical.

13

INCREASE SALES WITH THE ENERGETIC DRIVER CUSTOMER

DON'T WASTE THEIR TIME

The most common complaint Energetic Drivers have about salespeople is that we frequently waste their time.

When you meet, there are six mistakes to avoid with Energetic Drivers, mistakes that frustrate them and make them feel like you wasted their time.

First, fail to know enough about the customer's business or needs. Second, start off with a lot of small talk. Third, ask them pointless questions. The fourth mistake is trying (in vain) to communicate a value proposition that fits everyone instead of tailoring it to their unique problem or opportunity. Fifth, talk too much or take too much time to explain details. Sixth, bring no value to the discussion, leaving them with no useful insights or information other than what they already know.

Mistakes like these might cost you the sale because Energetic Drivers are impatient and results-driven and will quickly move on to something else.

THINK TWICE BEFORE GIVING THEM A TAKE-IT-OR-LEAVE-IT SOLUTION

Tom had been in sales for nearly a decade and was usually successful. However, when he didn't take the time to read and adapt his approach to a customer's Energetic Driver style but presented them with his one-size-fits-all solution instead, Tom lost the sale.

Energetic Drivers resist even the slightest sales pressure, and when Tom presented the solution but failed to present or discuss the alternatives, they weren't comfortable with his approach.

Tom should have given the customer some options or worked with them to understand the total value of his solution that fit their needs better. Instead, he pushed them away with what came off as a cookie-cutter approach.

Give these buyers plenty of options and always leave space for ongoing discussion to understand their unique needs and how you can best achieve their goals.

BE DIRECT AND AVOID SMALL TALK

"Start at the end of what you want to say," is an old saying that definitely applies. You can mesh more easily with them if you speak concisely and emphasize outcomes rather than data or details. The key to selling to Energetic Driver customers is to communicate in a way that makes them respect your competence and feel comfortable that you truly understand their needs.

The first step you should take is to focus early and often on needs discovery. You must be organized and prepared. Ask intelligent questions. Move through the discussion at their pace and match their assertive, commanding nature with a confident tone of your own.

After a thorough needs discovery, tailor a value proposition to satisfy their unique goals and get the desired results they want. Definitely, this is the best way to win their support.

An Energetic Driver will have a no-nonsense approach to the decision and an emphasis on results. Their frank and fast-paced style might make you uncomfortable if you're not prepared.

CREATE CLEAR, FORWARD-MOVING SALES CALL GOALS

One of the most frequent selling mistakes with Energetic Drivers is to set sales call goals that are too low.

When football teams break from the huddle, they want more than to hike the ball. They want to advance the ball down the field and score. Similarly, having clear, aggressive sales call goals with Energetic Drivers is crucial. There are three reasons for this.

First, Energetic Drivers are motivated to move projects forward and attack problems head-on. Second, they can be direct, forceful, and impatient. If you don't keep things moving and progressing, they may lose interest and move forward without you. Third, since they're geared to make faster decisions, your forward-moving mentality won't be uncomfortable; they'll actually respect and like it.

Early in the sales process, the most effective sales call goal you can have is to ask questions to help you thoroughly understand their problem or opportunity. What is it they want to achieve or solve? Why is it important to address this right now? Why did they want to talk with you?

Another important goal is to learn everything you can about their decision-making process, who's involved, and their specific role in deciding or influencing the purchase. Energetic Drivers might give the impression that they're the only decision influencer, but that's rarely the case in today's collaborative environment.

I'll add one more essential sales call goal: to identify and understand three potential needs that can give you an advantage in closing sales with Energetic Drivers. Learn about their known needs and probe for unrecognized or underprioritized needs. No matter how experienced or knowledgeable your Energetic Driver customer, they may fail to see or prioritize all aspects of the purchase. Your efforts to meet their total needs will earn their respect and trust.

TREAD SOFTLY ON THEIR MISTAKES

A tendency to refuse to see how they could be wrong is one of the Energetic Driver's potential shortcomings, as described earlier in this book.

When your customer is an Energetic Driver, this presents a potentially touchy selling problem. You might have to point out their mistake or assumption, and if so, you'll want to give them an out.

My first-hand experience with this situation came during an engagement with a sales executive and client. Upon completion of my salesforce interviews, he claimed he wanted to move forward. When I discovered a fundamental sales management error on his part that would likely result in lost sales going forward, I didn't protect his ego when I addressed it with him. He didn't like it, and wouldn't communicate with me for months.

Since that unfortunate debacle, I developed five steps to help break down uncomfortable feedback into something an Energetic Driver can accept and use. First, you should present your insights through a series of questions to get them thinking. I like questions that allow them to use their perspective on a problem or unforeseen possible outcome. Then present a well-organized and concise explanation of your concern. Because logic suits them well, they welcome alternative solutions or ideas that will produce superior results.

The second step is to avoid dictating the solution. Instead, show them how your recommendation can deliver the desired results. Help them make the idea their own by asking for their opinion.

The third step is to give them time to absorb the information you share. Even if they're ready to make quick decisions, they may need time to figure out how to communicate the changes to others.

The fourth step is to make sure you're ready to challenge the viewpoints of an Energetic Driver. Question their ideas and perspectives without criticizing them personally. When you disagree, take issue with the facts, not the person.

For the fifth step, it's crucial to recognize the individual as a unique person. Energetic Drivers share common traits, but their decision-making style can vary significantly in urgency, control, and self-protection. Your goal is to read the customer and adapt to each person's preferences.

GIVE THEM A COMPELLING REASON

When making changes, Energetic Drivers can be naive and shortsighted because they can't easily see their weaknesses.

Timothy worked for a company that hired me to provide ongoing customized coaching. The challenge he faced was convincing prospects to grant him an appointment. Timothy claimed that prospects were already loyal to the competition. He told me that getting in the door had become impossible. He spent the next twenty minutes trying to convince me.

Actually, he couldn't get an appointment because he didn't offer a strong enough reason. It's not that Energetic Drivers don't want to see salespeople, it's that they only meet with salespeople who convince them they'll gain something worthwhile for the time investment.

I explained to him, "Customers are very busy, and they'll look for any excuse to delete your email or voicemail message or to say they don't have time right now to meet but call them back in six months. Truth is, customers want to get rid of you because they think, based on the reason you offered, that you'll waste their time."

Timothy said, "So how do I break through? How do I get them to have a conversation with me?"

I said, "What would make you unlock your door and let someone you don't know into your house?"

Timothy thought for a moment. "They'd need to give me a convincing reason to have something I want."

"Exactly," I said. "Same thing when you try to land an appointment with an Energetic Driver. You must give them a 'compelling reason' why they should let you have their valuable time."

In the following sessions, we worked on his approach. A few weeks later, he got an appointment with a big prospect who had previously denied him.

Timothy was dealing with an Energetic Driver, but the 'compelling reason' strategy can work with any buyer.

AVOID EXAGGERATION

One of our clients in the medical manufacturing sector had a salesman embellish their product with a surgeon decision-maker at a hospital. As soon as the salesman told the surgeon, "Our surgical tool is unbendable," the surgeon grabbed the tool from the salesman, reached down, slid the tool head under one corner of his heavy desk, and pulled, lifting the desk several inches. Withdrawing the badly bent surgical tool, he firmly said, "I don't think it's unbendable!" He immediately escorted the overzealous salesman out the door and banished him from ever calling on his department again.

Avoid over-emphasizing your product's benefits with Energetic Drivers. Give them the pros and cons, and explain the outcomes objectively, then provide them with the space and time to decide for themselves. Also, don't use well-worn cliches like, "I think this is perfect for you" or "I know exactly what you need." You can ruin relationship and trust if you oversell.

DO YOUR HOMEWORK, RUN THE NUMBERS, AND QUANTIFY THE VALUE

The term "elevator pitch" goes back to the early 1850s when the Otis Elevator company's founder, Elisha Otis, rented a large convention hall and, with a working demonstration, made a convincing pitch for his invention, which was a reliable braking system for elevators.

In many American city buildings, the elevators of the time used an unreliable system of ropes and pulleys to stop the crudely designed elevators. If the cable snapped, the elevator plunged to the ground, injuring or killing people.

Since Otis successfully communicated his pitch to customers, we can learn from his approach. There's a catch, however. As a sign of our highly competitive times, you must run the numbers and quantify the value of your solution to differentiate your value from the competition. Energetic Drivers will not take the time necessary to do this for themselves. They rely on you to provide informed insights and proof to differentiate your value convincingly.

STAY OUT OF "THE COMMODITY COFFIN"

The "commodity coffin" effect happens when a customer sees our product or service as too similar to the competition. Since they can't see how our offering differs, they commoditize it.

Because Energetic Drivers are ambitious, goal-oriented, and highly treasure results, they expect salespeople to explain precisely how your solution will increase revenue, decrease costs, boost productivity, or other values that determine their decision. If you can't, you'll end up in the commodity coffin.

Without understanding their biggest concerns, you'll have trouble articulating a compelling value proposition and differentiating yourself. And you'll end up in the commodity coffin.

Once you're in the commodity coffin, their main goal is to get your lowest price — cheaper.

Sadly, most salespeople end up in the commodity coffin. That doesn't have to be the case. Follow these three steps to be distinct in the minds of these customers.

First, make sure you know the total value of what you're selling. Second, appeal to their results-driven nature and show them how your solution will help them reach their goals. The third step is to ask intelligent questions that will shift their thinking, and break through entrenched assumptions.

Your goal is to identify at least one need or problem they didn't recognize or which they underprioritized before talking with you. When you do, you won't have to ask them to see your solution in a brighter light. They already will.

DON'T DO INFORMATION AVALANCHES WHEN PRESENTING

Driven, focused decision influencers want things to move quickly, so they typically don't like deep dives into technical or analytical matters.

Energetic Drivers are highly focused and can be impatient if they feel their time is being wasted. You should give them just enough info to pique their interest, but it has to be info they want. Be concise, and don't go on and on about a product's features or advantages. Get straight to the points that matter most to them and highlight your solution's main benefits.

Ask questions and let their answers guide you to what they want to hear. Their need for control can be intense. By being selective about the information you emphasize, you make good use of their time and give them a feeling of control over the dialogue.

Goal-oriented buyers like Energetic Drivers are always looking to achieve their desired outcomes, so they want to know how your product or service will help them. Keep incidental information to a minimum, and emphasize how your solution impacts their goals.

COMMUNICATE WITH CONFIDENCE AND COMPETENCE

When meeting with an Energetic Driver, communicating directly and competently is essential. In my experience, there are two things to avoid in this area.

First, avoid trying to sound like you're an expert on a topic if you aren't because they'll pick it up quickly. Second, avoid making personal promises or assurances, even if you're attempting to be funny because Energetic Drivers become skeptical or dismissive quickly.

For example, when my wife and I were shopping for a car, we encountered a long-winded salesman who liked using well-rehearsed phrases and corny one-liners. The Energetic Driver traits in me engaged immediately, and I began challenging his remarks with questions.

When he said, "I'll tell you one thing, the engine runs so smoothly you could balance a quarter on it," I nearly laughed in his face. "I want to see that," I replied. He chuckled nervously. "No, I'm not joking. I want to see you do that," I said.

He hemmed and hawed for several moments, and I finally let him out of his embarrassing trap. We left the dealership and bought a car elsewhere. Confidence is critical with the Energetic Driver, but you must also demonstrate sincere competence to earn trust.

BUILD THE RELATIONSHIP GRADUALLY

Don't try to build a relationship too fast. The best way to develop a relationship with an Energetic Driver is to not waste their time, get to the point, focus on how they can get the results they want, know what you're talking about, value their viewpoints, be an excellent listener, and demonstrate competence. That's what builds rapport and credibility fast.

Once they like you, they'll be more open to developing relationships. They might ask you questions like, "How long have you been here?" or "What did you do before this?"

Build a relationship with Energetic Drivers by practicing the above effective habits and avoiding these three mistakes. First, don't make small talk when it's almost certain that the customer doesn't want to hear it.

Second, never assume you've earned personal rapport because of your company's brand image. I made this mistake as a new salesperson for a major chemical brand until one buyer told me, "I don't give a $%& what big company you work for." Respect is earned, and rapport is built on the customer's terms, not yours.

Third, keep in mind that false flattery won't gain you any points with them. Stick to more important discussion and save your compliments for when they have a legitimate reason for being stated.

ASK BREAKTHROUGH QUESTIONS

"People must think before they buy, and questions make them think." While this applies to all customers, the Energetic Driver and Numbers Thinker are most easily influenced by a thought-provoking question, especially if they think it will lead to better results or decisions.

Sales manager Jeffrey noticed a slump in his team's sales to high net-worth customers, so we reviewed their discovery questions and found they were dull and ineffective. As soon as we taught his sellers to think outside the box to break through the assumptions and status quo thinking and how their high net-worth customers usually look at purchase decisions - the team saw dramatic increases in closing rates.

Developing breakthrough questions takes time and effort, but the results are worth it. Check out the questions at the end of this chapter for possible breakthrough questions you might use.

TAILOR FIT SOLUTIONS TO VALUES

During my twenties, I worked fundraising for a national nonprofit. My boss worked with me on ways to communicate and build rapport with executives at high levels of decision-making power. Since he was good at interacting with our clients, and since decisions about significant contributions were made by a C-level executive, my boss got me ready for the challenge.

He told me to be direct and concise and to keep a pace and poise that matched the executive. And to talk to their "hot buttons," or main decision drivers.

I remember my interaction with the CEO of a big pharmaceutical company. When I asked for a large donation, he sized me up for a few awkward moments, and then he pulled out his checkbook and wrote a check for the entire sum!

Undoubtedly, we had previously built a positive relationship, and obviously, he was confident in our cause. But he also liked how our organization's purpose and activities aligned with his company's values — something I covered several times in earlier meetings.

Describing how you'll help Energetic Drivers reach their goals by aligning with what they value is critical to their decisive nature.

POSSIBLE QUESTIONS TO ASK

When dealing with an Energetic Driver customer, ask succinct and direct questions that quickly get to the root of the buyer's needs, goals, and desired results. By asking thorough questions, you can gain insights that will help you adapt your value message to effectively fit their needs. For example:

1. What are your main goals and how would you potentially like us to help you accomplish them?
2. What's your timeline for this project, and how critical is it that the solution is implemented by then?
3. Which key performance indicators are most significant?
4. How is your current supplier ensuring you they can produce these results in the future?
5. What are your most pressing challenges, and what are the consequences if they aren't solved adequately? How can we solve them for you?
6. What are the consequences if the solution you buy doesn't work like you need?
7. What would you most like to improve or change from the previous solutions you've tried?
8. How do you measure ROI when it comes to purchasing products/services?
9. What kind of priority does this project have for you? Your company?
10. How are you going to measure the impact my product/service will make for your situation?

TOP 10 CHAPTER HIGHLIGHTS

1. Be direct, avoid small talk unless they initiate.
2. Be organized, present ideas confidently and with a logical flow.
3. Focus on results, provide sufficient options.
4. Don't do "information avalanches."
5. If you disagree, differ with facts, not the person.
6. Tailor fit solutions to fit specific problems.
7. Don't use trite lines like, "I feel this is perfect for you," or, "I know exactly what you need."
8. Answer questions or objections directly.
9. Be ready to accelerate the pace to keep up with their fast-acting preferences.
10. Ask insightful, thought-provoking questions that both demonstrate and expand your understanding of their needs. Listen to their answers with concentration.

14

⋀⋀ UNDERSTAND THE LIKABLE COMMUNICATOR CUSTOMER

Likable Communicators often greet people with enthusiasm and excitement, use big facial expressions or exaggerated handshakes, and engage in light banter as they introduce themselves.

They tend to appear self-assured and might make bold or amplified statements about their lives and accomplishments. During small talk, a Likable Communicator will likely be enthusiastic to participate. While they might ramble on for a while without stopping to think about the time, you can easily redirect them with a guided question.

Likable Communicators are talkative, might tell stories, and their tone often changes when they get excited. They're usually confident and comfortable speaking their minds without fear of judgment. They tend to like being the center of attention.

Likable Communicators are adept at interacting with others because they're friendly and outgoing. At times they may try too hard to get and keep people's attention. However, that doesn't mean they aren't concerned about others' opinions. It's just that they can act in more self-directed attention ways than some personalities like.

How to Spot a Likable Communicator In 4 Minutes:

- Greets people eagerly, welcoming, may engage in light banter or small talk.
- Uses open gestures, active facial expressions, expressive body language.
- Talkative, often speaks the loudest and most constantly in a group.
- May stray off the purpose of the communication, lose track of time.
- May lean forward or close physical distance.
- Action-based, faster pace desired.
- Optimistic, enthusiastic attitude, positive approach to things.

Additional Behavior to Watch:

- Eager to create relationships.
- Takes an upbeat, positive approach to how they view or deal with issues.
- Shows an interest in exciting new products and outcomes.
- Willingness to be an open book on their likes and dislikes or needs.
- Communications, whether verbal or written, are usually wordy.
- Email/texting: wordy, colorful, dynamic language, and may inject humor or personality; uses exclamation points or emoticons to express emotion.

ADAPT TO THE LIKABLE COMMUNICATOR CUSTOMER

Think about how your style might best adapt to the Likable Communicator's style.

If you're an Energetic Driver: You like to get straight to the point. But Likable Communicators enjoy small talk and are less concerned with focusing on business alone. When you ask them a question, you might not want their wordy answers, but you should be attentive and give them time to finish. Use questions that will guide them back onto the issue. If necessary, slow down, since they might not decide as fast as you do. Choose your words carefully. Being too direct or blunt can make them uncomfortable with you.

If you're a Likable Communicator: You'll connect with them quickly. However, don't spend too much time on small talk, even though you both enjoy it, because getting sidetracked could make a thirty-minute meeting turn into a ninety-minute one. You understand better than most why they prioritize relationships in their personal and professional lives. They also value the impact their choices will have on others. While they can be quick decision-makers, you know it's unwise to pressure them into a decision, because they'll resist.

If you're an Obliging Helper: Your relaxed, easygoing personality will make them feel comfortable sharing their ideas and opinions with you. However, remember they also want to see your enthusiasm for the product. Because they're more impulsive, be ready if they're inclined to make decisions faster than you think. Be sure to ask questions that challenge them to see things differently and encourage them to express their opinions and ideas. Try to keep your part of the discussion short so they have plenty of opportunity to be an open book about their needs and desires.

If you're a Numbers Thinker: You approach decision-making with skepticism, are methodical, and make decisions slowly because you want to be highly accurate. While you may appreciate complex decision-making, they have a low tolerance for it because they like to make decisions more quickly and rely on feelings of confidence and positivity toward a particular product. Be enthusiastic about your product's value, and show it. Learn to adapt to the fact that they might want less information than you think is needed. They'll prefer to share their perspective rather than regularly hear yours, so ask, don't tell.

15

✎ INCREASE SALES WITH THE LIKABLE COMMUNICATOR CUSTOMER

ANTICIPATE THEIR NATURAL TENDENCIES

The phrase "different strokes for different folks" often refers to the idea that people have varying preferences and styles.

Not everyone is comfortable selling to Likable Communicators. For instance, there's John, a Numbers Thinker, goal-driven salesman with three decades of experience who prides himself on winning deals. But what sellers like John don't understand as well as they should is that every customer has potentially different preferences for communication, pace, and relatability.

In my coaching with John, he struggled to adapt to the Likable Communicator because he had the habit of selling to people how he would want to be sold.

To understand the Likable Communicator, keep four of their strongest tendencies in mind. First of all, they want the big picture before you get into details. They want to know how you do business and who you are.

Second, they talk a lot and may speak for a long time. Once trust and rapport are established, they want meaningful interaction to characterize the relationship. They'll probably lean forward, show enthusiasm, or use bold gestures when they're passionate about their thoughts.

Third, Likable Communicators are relational, but ultimately, they want their business to succeed. To be effective with them, you need to balance the relational and the results sides of the opportunity.

Finally, if they lack experience or confidence in an area, your supportive actions and reinforcement of their questions and opinions will increase receptivity to your message.

DEVELOP TRUST AND RAPPORT

Build trust and rapport with Likable Communicators as early as possible. It's a way of establishing the relationship, showing you understand their needs and what they expect from you. Trustworthiness isn't just key to securing deals with them, it's also vital if you want them to introduce you to other decision-makers who can help you close the deal.

Making the Likable Communicator comfortable with your approach will be difficult if your style is standoffish or too businesslike. One way to create an appealing approach with them is to allow time for small talk, but don't overdo it. Spending a few minutes talking about something other than strictly business might be all they need to develop comfort with you.

You can also build trust and rapport with the Likable Communicator by asking engaging questions, discussing their opinions and ideas, listening with interest, and incorporating their language into your communications, especially the value proposition.

LIMIT THE DETAILS, BUT MAKE YOUR POINTS STICK

Jane was ready to sell her product to Brian, a big prospect account. She researched the account, knew what she wanted to convey, and was mentally prepared. However, Jane later admitted she spent too much time on the details.

Rather than giving him a comprehensive overview, Brian just wanted the most pertinent information. Jane failed to adapt to his information preferences, and she lost the sale.

With the Likable Communicator, you shouldn't give too much detail. It'd be best to layer in detail as needed rather than do a data dump.

Use these three strategies with your Likable Communicator. First, summarize the facts and figures and ask them how they think it affects their goals. Second, ensure that the details you share tie back to their needs or concerns by saying something like, "You said you were worried about efficiency and..." or try saying, "If I understood you right, you felt that our product was too..." And third, recap the most important points from your conversation periodically. This gives them a chance to clarify things.

ASK QUESTIONS THAT LEAD TO SOLUTIONS

When selling to someone who's a Likable Communicator, ask questions that excite the customer and make them want to talk about their situation. Ask the customer about their primary goals, why they're so interested in changing things, seeing improvements, or how they'll feel when they accomplish the objective.

By posing open-ended questions that focus on the customer's goals and motivations rather than emphasizing your product's features or details, you create more interest and receptivity to your value message.

For example, Teresa sells computer systems for business applications. She improved her results with Likable Communicators when instead of concentrating on detailed specs or technical points about the product, she asked, "What sparked your interest in getting a new system for your business?" or "What do you envision achieving with this new system?"

By encouraging the expressive buyer to share their purchase motivations, she created credibility and rapport while identifying insights on the buyer's decision that Teresa could use to guide her to a close.

If you're dealing with Likable Communicators, ask questions like, "What do you hope this purchase will achieve?" or "What will make you feel most satisfied six months from now?" Such questions reinforce Likable Communicator's natural optimism toward a challenge or issue and what you can offer them, leading to more candid answers.

REDIRECT THEIR DIALOGUE WITH QUESTIONS

They're called expressive for a reason. They love to talk, and sometimes it's too much.

To rein in their words, use *redirect questions* that stimulate dialogue while keeping them focused on the meeting's objectives. You can achieve positive results using this technique, and it's easy to master.

Here's an exercise I use with my coaching clients. I give them a template of redirect questions, like, "That's interesting, how did that affect your operations?" or "I didn't realize that. What do you think will be needed most when it comes to quality on this project?" Or, you can say, "That's helpful for me to know. So, let me ask you, what are the most important benefits you need to gain from this purchase?"

Next, modify these questions to fit your style, and then get yourself comfortable using them through practice or roleplaying. Seamlessly integrating them into your dialogue will encourage buyers to provide you more information about their decision drivers, giving you vital information for making your case.

SHOW OUTWARD ENTHUSIASM

For Likable Communicators to take you seriously, you should show genuine energy and enthusiasm for your products or services. They expect it.

Tom was the senior vice president of a company and a long-time client. When we talked by phone one afternoon about possible training, I made a mistake with his personality style and paid for it. "You don't seem very excited about talking about this training today," Tom said five minutes into our conversation. I shot out of my chair and tried to compose myself by saying something clever. Because he was a Likable Communicator, I knew my lack of energy and enthusiasm was a turn-off.

I had just come off a long trip and wasn't my upbeat, energetic self, but my mistake was that I didn't prepare myself for his personality style needs either. Fortunately, Tom knew this interaction wasn't regular for me, so he overlooked it because I had a lot of trust and credibility with him. But could you imagine the consequences if this had happened to a new, prospective client?

READ THE CLUES

Apparently, the phrase "showing their true colors" came from sailing. Ships would fly a flag of a friendly nation to approach an enemy ship without being suspicious. When they got within range, though, they revealed their true flag and attacked. They called it "showing their true colors."

Likable Communicators are easy to spot because, unlike those ships that used deceptive tactics, they consistently act the way they're supposed to. In that sense, they're an open book, but if you don't look for the signals, you'll miss out on connecting and communicating successfully. I'll give you an example.

I was with Roger, a field support salesperson I'd just started coaching because his sales never took off. When Roger called on a high-value prospect, the man's energetic gestures and the excitement in his voice were strong cues, but so were his friendly and outgoing greeting and talkative nature. Unfortunately, Roger didn't notice or adapt his numbers-oriented, stiff approach and failed to ask enough questions to get the man to share important information.

Since Roger never engaged his customer, the customer quickly lost interest. Not only did he not buy, but he also never agreed to meet again.

Likable Communicators aren't afraid to show their true colors, but you've got to notice and adjust your approach.

USE CASE STUDIES AND TESTIMONIALS

Jamie, an equipment salesman, once tried to sell to a well-known business owner with decades of experience. In addition to being a shrewd businessman, the customer was highly expressive in his personality.

In spite of meeting twice with him, the owner wasn't convinced the product would work and make a decent return for the company. Jamie kept going with his best sales pitch and slide deck for one more try. A wealth of knowledge and an understanding of the client's industry allowed him to talk about the product's performance, emphasizing how it'd boost revenue and transform operations.

However, the business owner wasn't convinced, and he eventually backed off, explaining he couldn't commit. He had lots of questions about durability, compatibility with existing systems, and technical support before committing.

During a win-loss review with the buyer, Jamie realized the customer understood his value. But his oversight was that he didn't talk to the business owner about what kind of proof he needed that Jamie's product would deliver as promised.

The hard lesson Jamie learned was that expressive types often need hard proof before they commit to a purchase, so it was his job to figure out the kind of proof they wanted and boost their confidence in choosing his solution over others.

LISTEN

A Likable Communicator can jump from topic to topic because they get excited about what they want to say, making attentive listening harder. There are five actions that will improve your listening skills with expressive people.

First, just listen to what the person has to say. When appropriate, nod your head and add quick comments like "Good point" or "Interesting, tell me more about that." (Remember to use the redirect questions discussed earlier when the person becomes too talkative.)

Second, avoid distractions from the environment, such as people passing by the door, coworkers interrupting, office chatter, phone calls, and decision influencers joining unplanned.

Third, turn off your cell phone and other electronics that create distractions.

Fourth, don't fidget with a pen, pencil, notebook, or crutch. It lowers your listening effectiveness and might make you miss something of importance.

Fifth, watch out for drifting attention and daydreaming. For instance, I recently assisted a very experienced salesperson in closing more deals by differentiating product value. On one call, the buyer casually mentioned a company initiative affecting his department. His comment seemed off-handed, and the salesman didn't hear it since he was too busy thinking about what he would say next. The customer mentioned it again, but the salesman missed seeing its significance because he wasn't listening carefully, allowing his mind to drift.

Studies consistently show that listening skills are one of the main differentiators separating high-performing salespeople from average producers. Because expressive customers are big talkers, you must have intense listening skills to identify needs accurately and close deals.

ASK BREAKTHROUGH QUESTIONS

With a Likable Communicator, using a breakthrough question might be best explained with an example.

I'd previously provided sales and customer service training for a well-known boat manufacturer, so Michael, the new service director, wanted to meet with me. Michael was friendly and talkative. After asking him several open-ended questions, I eventually asked this breakthrough question, "Michael, how long do you want customer service training to last?"

Michael hadn't been asked that before. This challenged his entrenched, status quo approach to fill training hours rather than focusing on ROI. After we talked about delivering training that lasts versus training hours per employee, he got it.

Ultimately, he loved the results, and my company's revenues increased with long-term engagements. Asking the right questions that get the customer thinking in new ways can lead to a win-win for you and your client.

Start by understanding your Likable Communicator's goals and needs, then move on to questions that turn the discussion into one of value. For example, ask, "Have you considered the advantages of X and how it can accelerate desired results?" Or say, "What are the top three challenges you want to solve?" You can improve your persuasiveness by asking questions like these (with any personality style) since they can help your buyer prioritize desired outcomes.

You want expressive-type customers to think differently instead of using standard approaches that might hold them back from better results, and using breakthrough questions is the key.

WATCH FOR SIGNS OF APPROVAL

Watch their behavior when you meet them. Pay attention to three things.

When they talk to others in the room or during a video conference, pay attention to their tone and body language. If they're interested or have strong feelings, the tone of voice should be friendly, even chummy. You'll find their body language more open if they get excited about your product than if they remain closed-off.

The second thing they'll do is introduce you to others at their company and tell them about your solution. It's a good sign. They might be starting to trust you. It could also mean they like you. The fact that you're moving up their list doesn't necessarily mean you've clinched the sale, though.

Thirdly, they might verbalize their approval by saying, "I think you have our best interests in mind," or, "I really like your approach, and I think this is going to work out nicely!" They might introduce you to a colleague. So, they might say, "This is Susan, the salesperson I've been telling you about, and I feel her solution is perfect and I'm really excited about it."

Even though they don't realize it, they're helping you plan your closing strategy.

POSSIBLE QUESTIONS TO ASK

Ask questions that energize the customer and make them want to discuss their situation. They usually like to talk about their primary goals, why they're so interested in improving things, making changes, or how they'll feel when they achieve the desired results. Try asking questions like the following by changing them to fit your style and your customer's situation.

1. What are your goals or vision for this project?
2. What kind of information would be helpful when considering this purchase?
3. How does the problem or opportunity impact operations, employees, or customers?
4. What solutions are you personally leaning toward? Why?
5. In addition to price, what are the main criteria/factors driving your decision? Get specifics.
6. On a scale of 1-10, how high is your commitment to solving this operational problem?
7. What has been your experience with similar products in the past? Which ones didn't work, and how'd you feel about them?
8. Which aspects of our product create the most excitement or interest for you? (Or, What will excite you most when this problem is solved?)
9. Based on what you've seen so far, how comfortable (or confident) are you that our product will help you achieve your goals?
10. How are you going to measure the impact my product/service will make for your situation?

TOP 10 CHAPTER HIGHLIGHTS

1. Develop credibility, trust, and likability early.
2. Limit the details; get to the main selling points.
3. Let them talk.
4. Redirect with questions to keep them on topic.
5. Show enthusiasm/energy for your product or service.
6. Develop rapport; let them get to know you.
7. Provide impressive testimonials and case studies.
8. Be an excellent listener; verbally and nonverbally respond.
9. Watch for signs of approval.
10. Ask open-ended questions focusing on the customer's goals and motivations rather than concentrating too much on your product's features or details.

16

⌁ UNDERSTAND THE OBLIGING HELPER CUSTOMER

Meeting an Obliging Helper is a refreshing experience. You'll be welcomed with open arms, meaningful eye contact, and a regular smile.

You can expect polite conversation, a quiet demeanor, and thoughtful answers to your questions. The one exception is when they withhold their true feelings or thoughts to avoid conflict.

When you get to know an Obliging Helper, rest assured that their radiating warmth and friendliness are genuine. They generally like making small talk about getting to know each other better. They want to know about your family, friends, hobbies, and interests, usually avoiding things that might cause disagreement.

Slow and steady is how Obliging Helpers communicate verbally, so don't rush or interrupt them. Instead, give them the time and silence to express themselves completely. They tend to listen carefully and show their understanding with brief acknowledgment and facial expressions.

Obliging Helpers might avoid attention-seeking activities or dominant roles and instead opt for a more supportive role that facilitates the entire team's engagement.

How to Spot an Obliging Helper In 4 Minutes:

- Greets people in a warm, cheerful manner and smiles.
- Soft-spoken, has an easygoing, leisurely pace.
- Attentive listener, patient.
- Indecisive, cautious, seeks minimal risk or change.
- Relationship-centered, accepting, and trusting of others.
- Requires ample time to commit.

Additional Behavior to Watch:

- Can mask their true feelings effortlessly.
- Methodical approach to decision-making.
- Accommodating, supportive, and avoids challenging others.
- Wants to work with team members and collaborate on decisions.
- Seeks out stable, reliable outcomes.
- Doesn't want to disappoint and may avoid needed change.
- Loves choices but hates choosing.
- Email/texting: courteous tone; expresses support, helpfulness, or appreciation; can be detailed and thorough with facts and examples; expect cordial language, patience, and cooperation towards people and situations; often end as they begin, with kind words.

ADAPT TO THE OBLIGING HELPER'S NEEDS

Consider how your style might best adapt to the Obliging Helper's style.

If you're an Energetic Driver, you want discussions to move along, but you'd be better off slowing down and giving them time to think things through. The Obliging Helper buying style values trust and relationships and wants to know you because it influences their decision. Don't be too pushy and direct the conversation to the point where you overpower them. Let Obliging Helper customers share their views while you listen attentively. Look for subtle reservations or disagreements. They'll camouflage most emotions with an air of agreement.

If you're a Likable Communicator, you share their need for personal interaction and relationships. They commonly drag their feet on deciding, especially if they feel under pressure or sense too much risk. Give them time to weigh the options, think through your solution, and slow things down to their liking. To build trust, ask more questions instead of providing so much information. In general, dial down your enthusiasm to ensure they have ample opportunity to express their feelings. Never assume silence indicates agreement.

If you're an Obliging Helper, your main characteristics are similar to theirs, so you'll feel comfortable working with them. Take caution, however, since you can easily get lost in the relationship and might overlook your main objective to win the deal. Obliging Helpers working together can get easily sidetracked and have lengthy encounters that use considerable time, slowing the sales process. You can guide the conversation back on track with questions by directly showing interest in your buyer's feelings about purchasing your product. You can also offer reassurances, guarantees, and support, which you know will encourage them to make the right decision.

If you're a Numbers Thinker, you'll want to gather data before making specific recommendations. For the Obliging Helper customer to feel comfortable with the decision, they need reassurance, peace of mind, and supportive collaboration with you and others. Your thoroughness and willingness to cater to their information needs make them more likely to feel they're making the right choice and can trust you. Too much emphasis on data is a turn off, so balance your focus on information with their preferences for only the most relevant, proof-worthy information.

17

INCREASE SALES WITH THE OBLIGING HELPER CUSTOMER

MEET FIVE NEEDS

Obliging Helpers have five fundamental communication and relationship needs that you want to find ways to satisfy.

First, friendly conversation builds a sense of connection and relationship. Because they appreciate knowing you, using a relaxed conversation style that allows open sharing of information and feelings will be received positively.

Second, they're motivated to help you understand their needs, and you can help them by asking questions that probe their feelings and thoughts, not just facts.

Third, they also prefer predictable, standard solutions. So, if your offering overwhelms them or they need clarification, create manageable goals for using your product, clear action steps, and smaller commitments that can be phased in over time.

Fourth, when they don't provide free-flowing feedback, be patient. To get better details, try scheduling more frequent but shorter meetings. Invest time in your pre-call planning to develop questions that fit their style. Support their views by using affirming comments and listening with comprehension.

Fifth, an Obliging Helper wants relevant proof to support your claims. They don't want an information avalanche. Instead, be selective and present honest evidence to lessen their concerns.

PIVOT AS QUICKLY AS YOU CAN

Nate is a client's account manager who's been through my training. He reads his customers' personality styles and does an excellent job adapting to fit their needs, even though sometimes he struggles with Obliging Helper type buyers. When this happens, Nate knows what makes them tick, how patiently one must turn skepticism into receptivity and trust, and how critical it is to build rapport early in the sales process.

Nate also knew from our training that he ultimately needed to turn the conversation away from features and price to a discussion focused on benefits and value. He achieved this by asking questions like, "I realize this is somewhat different from what you've used before. What potentially concerns you about my product?" or "How do I prove to your team that my product has all the benefits you'll need?"

Selling to the Obliging Helper decision-making style requires recognizing their traits quickly and pivoting your style just as fast to satisfy their preferences.

MAKE RAPPORT BUILDING A PRIORITY

Build rapport and connect with Obliging Helpers before discussing their situation or concerns.

Let's say, however, that you're too focused on business and don't take the time to establish a positive relationship. In that case, it will potentially impact their interest and you could lose the sale. I know. I've done it.

The mistake I made a few years ago was focusing on results rather than relationships when I first met a prospective client. I was in a busy season, and I let that affect how I approached the meeting. I knew better, but still blew it by allowing my nature to decide how I sold rather than adapting my approach to the priorities and tendencies of the decision-makers.

Selling to an Obliging Helper is challenging, particularly if you're a Numbers Thinker or Energetic Driver. While you might find building rapport and relating through conversation time-consuming or tiresome, they see it as a valuable use of time and feel energized by it.

LAYER YOUR INFORMATION AND SEEK MINOR AGREEMENTS

Obliging Helpers want to avoid making mistakes or losing the respect of their bosses or coworkers.

The trick is to get small agreements that make them feel more comfortable with the commitment. Here's how to make your layering approach successful: First, ask the right questions to get the necessary information that will allow you to tailor your value message to the customer's concerns.

Second, be clear about your value and how it aligns with achieving the customer's goals. If you can do this, you'll be more likely to persuade them that the risk they'll take on a purchase is minimal.

Third, find out what support materials the decision influencer would like to consider (case studies, testimonials, videos, other marketing info). Also, see if you can provide helpful information for their fellow decision influencers.

The fourth way is to make yourself and others available to answer questions. Set up a joint call or videoconference with any of your company's experts if the customer wishes so they feel comfortable committing.

You'll accomplish three things with a layering strategy: prevent unfounded fears about your products, show convincing results other customers have seen using your solutions, and give the buyer enough time to think things through with others before purchasing.

USE A METHODICAL APPROACH TO DISCUSS GOALS AND NEEDS

Obliging Helper buyers prefer to avoid sudden change or uncertainty. As the following story illustrates, your number one mistake is suddenly imposing anything new on them and assuming they'll support it.

During a coaching session, a professional services client told me about losing a repeat customer with whom he had an excellent relationship. My client recommended a new approach when the customer had a new project. Unfortunately, however, he failed to explain to her that he would still sell it as before through traditional channels, but she didn't fully understand the change in the approach. And since he didn't take the time to notice and handle her uneasiness, she awarded the project to someone else.

Let's compare his result to salesperson Jim's success closing his Obliging Helper customer. While he still convinced the customer to buy the novel, unique solution, he started by asking the right questions and used that information to discuss how his approach would meet their needs. Taking extra precautions to address possible reservations, he closed the deal flawlessly.

Keeping Obliging Helper engaged in a two-way conversation before introducing a new solution allows you to help them deal with conflicting feelings. And it gives them sufficient time to think about it.

USE FIVE STEPS WHEN SEVERAL PEOPLE INFLUENCE THE DECISION

In Obliging Helpers' opinion, collaborating with others is the best way to make good decisions.

Be careful! Getting others involved can result in delays, unnecessary changes to requirements or volumes, and muddying up the objectives.

Here are five ways to help your customers involve others while benefiting you. First, give them ample time to include others and get their support. Be open to working with anyone in the company who has a role in the decision.

Second, follow up on any contacts your Obliging Helper customer gives you and establish relationships with the decision influencers so that you have their support when it's time to decide.

Third, identify your customer's concerns or fears. Work to eliminate or minimize them.

Fourth, set interim checkpoints so you can see how the decision is progressing rather than waiting until they've decided. In this way, you can have some influence instead of assuming things are going fine, engage more people's support, and possibly guide the customer in how to accurately weigh competitor offerings with yours.

Fifth, make sure you're involved after the sale. Work with the decision-makers to be accessible for current and future needs.

USE MILESTONES TO GAUGE ACCEPTANCE

Christine, a client's sales representative, made numerous calls to her Obliging Helper customer but ultimately lost the sale. Christine told me, "I was fooled by the customer's remarks and friendly behavior, so I coasted to the finish and thought I could get the sale."

Christine acknowledged that her mistake relied on her gut instinct about the customer's interest. Obliging Helpers can be challenging to read, and identifying milestones in your sales process that must be accomplished with the prospect's actions will help prevent counting on the customer's easily-made promises — promises that might lead to a lost sale.

WORK WITH THEIR EASYGOING NATURE, NOT AGAINST IT

To increase your chances of winning an Obliging Helper customer's business, learn to work with their easygoing, modest, and cautious nature.

Stefan, a top producer in a large industry, told me how identifying his prospect's Obliging Helper nature and adjusting his style led to a big sale. It is an impressive story, and I think you'll see the value in it:

I met with the lead decision-maker for a big government contract and learned it was his first time leading a big purchase decision.

He invited my competitors and me to meet and tour the facility. As I toured the facility, I asked him thoughtful but easy questions. I tried to build a relationship with him, so I didn't initially pose too many challenging questions. When he asked me a question, I answered it relaxed, hoping to mirror his style. In addition, given his cautious nature, I looked for opportunities to sincerely encourage him in his role by complimenting his well-thought-out audit and implementation plan, etc.

During the tour, my competition asked hard, critical questions like, "Are you sure about that?" or made unfavorable remarks like, "I think this might work, but I have my doubts."

After my competitors pounded the buyer with relentless questions during the joint conference meeting, the customer became disengaged. He changed from being calm and relaxed to anxious and uncomfortable. I presented my proposal at a follow-up meeting. Even though my system cost over 30 percent more, and the customer had to modify the RFQ to align with my system's specifications, I closed the sale.

This is a remarkable example of how an Obliging Helper personality can assist you if they like your approach — including helping you fully understand their needs so that your solution aligns with their goals.

Getting the cooperation of Obliging Helper buyers is all about adapting throughout the entire sales process until you close.

HELP THEM TAKE THE INITIATIVE

There isn't anything wrong with Obliging Helpers' slow decision-making, it's just that they hate change.

Here are three ways to get your Obliging Helper buyer to take the initiative. The first thing to do is to ask questions that get them to think about why the decision is critical and should be made promptly.

Second, you must listen to and understand what they're saying. Listening shows your respect and interest in what they're trying to communicate. Use questions to clarify or confirm important information they share with you.

Third, speak their language. Listen carefully to find out what's driving their decision-making. Then, include the language they use in your communications. You can positively influence the decision by relating your value proposition to the customer's specific drivers.

DON'T MAKE OFF-HANDED STATEMENTS

Obliging Helper clients are known to respond poorly to subtle pressure or vain attempts to impress them. Here are a couple of examples.

The salesperson tells the prospect, "Yes, we're super busy right now, but we can take care of what you need." The customer says, "Well, if you're that busy, maybe I should go elsewhere because I don't want to face problems with poor service down the road."

Similarly, when a salesperson says, "Usually we only take on clients with a million or more in purchasing, but we'd love to help you this time," it raises doubts in their minds that the company will treat them like a priority — and it doesn't meet their cautious, stability-oriented nature. Alarms go off in their brain, asking questions like, "Why do they have that rule but then break it?" and, "Can they be trusted, believed?"

Off-handed remarks are risky. Be professional, use trust-building language, and give the Obliging Helper a sense that their business matters.

USE PERSISTENCE, DON'T GET DISCOURAGED

Belinda was one of the top software salespeople in her company. She was known for her tenacity and perseverance, which had landed her significant sales. She'd been trying to land a deal with a new client recently but wasn't getting anywhere. The top decision-maker at the company was in no hurry to see her and kept rejecting her requests for an appointment.

After two years of trying, Belinda finally managed to get an appointment with the decision-maker. She did this by sending him a series of clever emails and mailers that got his attention. When they finally met, she pitched him her software system, and he bought it!

Maybe you're familiar with Vince Lombardi's saying, "The man on top of the mountain didn't fall there." It's a good reminder that persistence, like Belinda's, is what you'll need to persuade an Obliging Helper who doesn't want to change.

GET A SERIES OF SMALL COMMITMENTS

Many Obliging Helper buyers, if not most, look for security and need several assurances before they agree to purchase. That's where knowledge of style preferences, and a little patience, will pay off.

To win over cautious Obliging Helpers and establish trust, the most effective approach may be to first gain a series of small commitments, which serves as a pathway to a successful sale.

This strategy proved effective for a small company in the oilfield services industry, where testimonials, case studies, and engaging technical experts helped the seller build credibility and rapport with decision-makers. The salesperson eventually closed the sale by securing incremental commitments during each successive step in the sales process.

WATCH FOR HIDDEN OBJECTIONS AND RESISTANCE

I participated in several joint sales calls with coaching client Larry in Houston. One situation made Larry realize he didn't take the time to notice the customer's style and adjust his approach. After discussing it, he said, "I didn't ask the right questions and missed the signs of skepticism and indifference toward my value message."

Larry's mistake is common when selling to Obliging Helpers, who, if they desire, can hide their genuine emotions and feelings.

You can get Obliging Helpers to talk and be more revealing about specific concerns or doubts by gently questioning them until they open up. There are three kinds of questions that work. First, clarify their meaning: "That's a great point. What do you mean by a prolonged process?"

Second, ask questions to expand on pertinent information, such as: "What does your conclusion depend on?" or "What are your typical parameters?" and "How do you feel about the current level of safety?"

Lastly, ask questions to learn about the motivation behind their beliefs, actions, or concerns: "Why's that a critical outcome for this project?" and "How'd you come to that conclusion?"

The Obliging Helper will appreciate such questions because they want to help, not hinder your efforts, and aren't opposed to being influenced if it leads to the best decision.

HELP THEM DEAL WITH COMPETING VIEWS

When several decision influencers are involved, each with a potentially different opinion about what product to purchase, you need a good strategy with your Obliging Helper.

The most effective way to deal with competing views is to engage others in the discussion with thoughtful, direct questions. For instance, you could ask, "Based on what we've talked about, what do you think the biggest benefits are for your company?" or "Based on the ROI case studies, does our product make sense to you?" and "Do you have a preference for one product over another?"

You can also go to the Obliging Helper for their support. Provide them with the value proposition you've created and ask, "What recommendations do you have to improve it so that I can make the most compelling case to your purchasing team?" Remember that the Obliging Helper aims to reach a decision that satisfies all parties. Thus, if they're convinced by your offering, they'll have a vested interest in seeing you make a convincing case.

Individuals may need to look beyond their departments' preferences and endorse the solution that offers the best overall value for the company. Your Obliging Helper contact may be willing to help you with that too.

BE AN ENGAGING LISTENER

The more comfortable an Obliging Helper becomes with you, the more willing they are to share information that can help you. Their style responds positively to good listening skills, including giving them regular verbal or nonverbal affirmation when you support their feedback.

When I met with prospective client Jerome, Vice President of a bank, at the end of our first meeting, he stood, shook my hand, and said, "You're a great listener. Has someone ever told you that?" I awkwardly told him they had and added, "Now, if I could just get my wife to think that!" We both chuckled.

Numerous studies have shown that listening is one of the primary skills separating top sales performers from average performers. Being a great listener with an Obliging Helper customer might be the only noticeable difference between you and your competition. And that can be enough to swing the deal your way because it builds trust and gives them the confidence that you understand their needs accurately.

Here are five ways to connect positively with Obliging Helper through listening. First, make steady eye contact, smile, and occasionally nod to show agreement and interest.

Second, ask questions flowing from the conversation to show that you prioritize what they say. An Obliging Helper likes it when you genuinely value their viewpoint.

The third thing you can do is ask questions to clarify or elaborate, like, "So, based on what you just said, how'd you fix that problem?" or "What impact did it have on your costs?" Or, "Why's that important to you?"

Fourth, repeat what they shared to ensure you get it: "Correct me if I'm wrong, but I heard you say there were two main reasons. Is that correct?"

Fifth, make comments to support their feedback, such as, "That's very interesting for me to know," or "Thank you for sharing that because I wasn't aware of..." An Obliging Helper customer responds to supportive statements by trying to think of other things you might find helpful. It builds stronger relationships, too.

POSSIBLE QUESTIONS TO ASK

To effectively sell to an Obliging Helper, you want to create an environment that encourages honest dialogue while building positive relationships. This requires asking questions that make the customer feel listened to and valued. Try asking questions like the following by changing them to fit your style and your customer's situation.

1. What are your top priorities or goals when it comes to this purchase?
2. What made you decide on this route?
3. We've discussed a lot of info about your needs and my product's capabilities. What aspects of our product sound like they can possibly benefit you the most?
4. Are there any specific capabilities or benefits you want from this project?
5. Do you have any concerns or reservations about my solution? Are there any other factors we haven't discussed that will influence your decision?
6. Are you loyal to any existing supplier relationships or partnerships for this purchase?

7. Are you involving the input of others in the decision? Is there a particular way I can help you help others understand my product and its value?

8. Do you know of anyone on your purchasing team who does not favor purchasing my product? How would you suggest that I work with them?

9. Does your business have any future opportunities that this decision could impact favorably or unfavorably?

10. How are you going to measure the impact my product/service will make for your situation?

TOP 10 CHAPTER HIGHLIGHTS

1. Use a relaxed approach.
2. Try to have a brief, friendly conversation before business.
3. Stress guarantees, testimonials, and facts.
4. Provide sufficient details and specifics to reassure them.
5. Support them in involving others in the decision.
6. Make value clear and reinforce it.
7. Don't pressure them to decide quickly; get a series of small commitments leading up to a purchase.
8. Introduce them to service staff, technical experts, and managers.
9. Be an excellent listener and use verbal and nonverbal responses.
10. Ask questions that can help build trust and rapport by showing genuine interest in meeting their needs with the best possible solution.

18

⟋ Understand the Numbers Thinker Customer

When meeting someone for the first time, a Numbers Thinker may appear reserved and cautious, with understated tones and body language. They can handle basic facts impeccably and often prefer to stick to concise speech unless they share some Likable Communicator tendencies.

While they may seem distant in conversations, it's essential not to be too quick to dismiss their contributions. Analytic thinking styles tend to slice up a situation and look at the individual parts, potentially overanalyzing to avoid being wrong. They may also ask questions that no one else thinks to ask, and they may be the first person in a meeting with several buyers to challenge your data, numbers, or conclusions.

Numbers Thinkers tend to avoid prolonged eye contact and frequently shift their body postures when asked questions about themselves or their views on matters. In terms of small talk, they'll need prodding from you to start up light conversation.

How to Spot a Numbers Thinker in 4 Minutes:
- Greets you formally, has a reserved demeanor, and shuns most small talk.
- Uses few to no gestures; avoids facial expressions.
- Deliberate speaking pace, to the point, objective, thorough.
- Skeptical of information and conclusions; wants proof.

- Responds cautiously and uses an unemotional approach to interaction.
- Good listening attentiveness and comprehension; writes things down.

Additional Behavior to Watch:
- Overanalyzes because they fear making wrong decisions; leans on perfectionism.
- Values facts and figures, scrutinizes the details, and is accuracy driven.
- Motivated to ask questions that clarify or confirm information.
- Interested in the process to get desired results; wants steps made clear.
- Reluctant risk-taker; slow decision-maker when change is required.
- Email/texting: is organized, precise, and detailed; uses facts and evidence with logical views; may be technical, offer solutions or instructions; focused on results; uses little emotion or pleasantries.

ADAPT TO NUMBERS THINKER CUSTOMER

Consider how your style might best adapt to the Numbers Thinker's style.

If You're an Energetic Driver, you might consider the analytical customer's intense drive for information and deliberate decision-making style challenging. Don't skip over details or facts. Numbers Thinkers must gain peace of mind because they don't make decisions as quickly as you do and won't appreciate forceful sales tactics. Instead of trying to change their style preferences, adapt to them. Most likely, they already know a lot about your company and its offerings, so find out what information they'd like and provide it.

If You're a Likable Communicator, you'll probably find selling to a Numbers Thinker difficult because their behavior can differ significantly from yours. First, be open to giving more facts and figures than you'd want if you were them. Rather than telling them what they need to know, which is more your style, ask them what they'd like to know. Don't be surprised if they're upfront with you when asking questions or identifying issues. Try not to get personal early on to break the ice. Stick to answering their questions and providing all the details they want. Analytical customers prioritize information and accuracy in their decisions and won't value your enthusiasm or positivity as much as others might.

If you're an Obliging Helper, you'll feel the urge to be personable and relational, but the analytical buyer mainly wants details and facts from you, not a friendly relationship. Sometimes they're intimidating because they question almost everything or ask questions you've never heard before. They're analyzing all the options and proving to themselves that your proposed actions will help. They think like giant outlines or spreadsheets, and it's your job to fill in the blanks. They're hard to read because they don't usually respond with enthusiasm or support. Unless you ask, you might not know if they're buying your product until the final decision is made.

If you're a Numbers Thinker, you'll feel naturally comfortable working with them because you prioritize order, organization, and details like they do. You'll also communicate more comfortably since your preference for seeing problems, finding solutions, and limiting risk will synchronize nicely. However, your desire to have things lined up exactly, such as all the details and charts, graphs, and lists before a decision can be reached, might risk losing the sale if your customer doesn't require all that information and is ready to close sooner. Don't assume that their analytical tendencies align perfectly with yours, especially since the chances are higher that they'll have a blend of traits that will present behavior differences.

19

⤳ Increase Sales with the Numbers Thinker Customer

DON'T GIVE YOUR "HOW GREAT WE ARE" PITCH

A client-CEO called me knowing that I coach against salespeople giving the "how great we are" pitch to prospective customers. He told me of an IT company that had recently met with his leadership team and that they had agreed to allow the company to provide a proposal for their IT needs.

After the meeting, the CEO sent the IT company a detailed internal report explaining their system's servers and needs. Three weeks later, the IT company came in for a follow-up meeting to close the deal. After several minutes of prolonged small talk, the IT company representatives dove into their "how great we are" spiel, including the systems they had worked on, their capabilities, and their go-to-market value proposition.

When the CEO asked if they had read the company's system's report he'd sent, they opened it up sheepishly and one of the representatives said, "LINUX? Do you use LINUX on your servers? We don't work with LINUX." The CEO, at that point, immediately showed them the door.

Analytic customers are demanding buyers to convince. Using 'pitchy' presentations or not doing your homework on their company will be a big turnoff. If you don't understand their needs precisely, you can kiss the deal goodbye.

DON'T BE REHEARSED OR ROBOTIC

I have a small business owner-client who's a Numbers Thinker, and he's super easy to read. He greets you formally, gets straight to the point, and regularly asks about the data and specifics behind any claims. His office is orderly and neat, and he's typically expressionless when talking or listening.

Salespeople rarely notice or adjust to his style needs, he tells me. Most of them rely on well-rehearsed lines like talking about the weather and the pictures on his wall. Or they'll ask pretentious questions like, "What keeps you up at night?" or this century's come-on line, "Tell me about your company."

Of course, they do all this meandering to warm him up for their one-size-fits-all sales pitch.

The business owner turns the table on them with challenging questions. "Where's your chart or backup proof of that?" "How would you know; you don't even know our volume?" "What does that have to do with my business?" "Do you even understand our business and its problems?"

Assuming you know what a Numbers Thinker wants or needs isn't good. Instead, ask thoughtful discovery questions, and use their answers to build your follow-up dialogue and questions. Tired, worn-out questions or leaning on well-rehearsed statements produce turndowns.

USE VISUALS IF YOU HAVE THEM – BUT ASK WHICH ONES

Three engineers I coach also serve as sales managers. They're interested in techniques and processes. As you might suspect, they like numbers and specifics. Their attentiveness intensifies whenever I reach for a chart or graph to illustrate something. If you watched from a hidden camera, you could see their eye contact brighten and you might notice them leaning forward to study the chart closer.

In a coaching session, one of the engineers/sales managers said, "You know me, I've never met a chart or graph I didn't like!"

Rather than risk being off-base on providing unhelpful information, ask a Numbers Thinker if you're unsure which charts, studies, testimonials, facts, research, or white papers they'd find helpful. They'll tell you.

HELP THEM DISCOVER AN UNRECOGNIZED OR UNDERPRIORITIZED NEED

A logical thinker analyzes the world around them, crunches the numbers, and looks for straightforward, predictable solutions.

Information, however, can trap them and make them blind to what might be the most effective overall solution. Thus, you'll want to get the Numbers Thinker to think about two other types of needs: unrecognized, which they don't perceive as a need, and undervalued, which they know is critical but don't prioritize highly enough.

In our coaching, we teach with a template of over one hundred proven sales questions that make your buyer think in new ways, because breaking through their status quo is the best way to get them to think differently. Good breakthrough questions often get positive reactions from buyers: "That's a great question," "No one has ever asked me that before," or "I've never thought about it that way."

Your analytical buyers, in particular, can benefit from effective questions because they can take into consideration new ideas or needs they didn't realize should be assessed. They can also re-prioritize their existing needs in your favor.

AVOID THE CURSES OF PRESUMPTION AND KNOWLEDGE

When you try to sell your value to a Numbers Thinker, avoid two traps.

The first trap, The Curse of Presumption, occurs when a salesperson presumes that the Numbers Thinker will make the right decision because they have a command of the facts and data and strive to make accurate decisions. It's surprising, but they might not be able to make an informed decision. They'll choose a competitor for reasons you never thought possible, such as failing to fully understand your solution's primary advantages.

As a second trap, The Curse of Knowledge occurs when the salesperson assumes that the Numbers Thinker will understand their product's benefits because they're so obvious or familiar to themselves. As soon as we understand the value of our product, we can't imagine someone not seeing it. This makes it easy to develop a positive bias about what we sell and think everyone can see its worth.

A study thirty years ago discovered that when people were asked to tap out the rhythm of the familiar *Happy Birthday* song on a table, and volunteers guessed the tune, less than three percent named the song correctly. Interestingly, before the volunteers guessed, the tappers predicted that over fifty percent would be correct. The warning is clear! It's dangerous to assume Numbers Thinkers will see our value as quickly or plainly as we do.

You can avoid the Curses of Presumption and Knowledge by taking nothing for granted when selling the Numbers Thinker on the value of your solution.

ASK QUESTIONS TO UNDERSTAND AND ADVANCE THE SALE

Alice, a sales representative with intense Likable Communicator tendencies, struggled to close a sale with a Numbers Thinker. She tried all kinds of strategies, but nothing worked. Her customer demanded all the details, logical explanations, and exact data before deciding.

I showed Alice how to ask Numbers Thinkers better questions, especially dialogue-generating questions that required more than yes or no answers. To her credit, she dug deeper into the details behind the customer's decision-making process: what kind of data did they need? What information would they find most helpful in making an accurate decision?

The change to better questions gave Alice improved insights into her buyer's purchasing motivations and the reasons for his caution. With this knowledge, Alice crafted a compelling value proposition supported with proof of her product's value, addressing every concern and answering every question her Numbers Thinker customer posed.

A Numbers Thinker gets their greatest pleasure in analyzing and planning accurately. But if you're not careful, they'll stall making the decision. Ask good questions to understand their perspective and to keep the sale advancing.

ASK THEM TO EXPLAIN

When I bought the radio station referred to earlier in the book, it had a ton of debt, and the goal was to increase sales fast. In order to close sales, we had to overcome a lot of obstacles, including a new talk format, a small signal, and an unproven ability to generate audience loyalty.

One of the business owners I tried to sell owned numerous copier shops, and his personality indicated strong Numbers Thinker and

Obliging Helper tendencies. After calling on him several times without any progress, I told him, "We can start your sports sponsorship for local high school sports in time for Friday night's game, but honestly, it seems like you have some concerns if I'm reading you correctly?" He was honest with me, and said, "Yes, you're right, I have concerns about advertising on your station because it's a brand-new format with no proven audience."

Knowing his true feelings enabled me to present our plan for how we were building listenership through our new local sports lineup. He liked the detailed plan and became our first sponsor.

Numbers Thinkers can be hard to pin down on their feelings and apprehensions. When they are, ask them to explain and really listen to their reasons.

ASK QUESTIONS TO DISCOVER THEIR TRUE FEELINGS

When we make a decision, our brain uses logic and emotion. And depending on the decision, we can experience both positive and negative emotions.

Analytic customers don't easily express their feelings. Even though they aren't exactly known for their transparency, they can still be surprisingly honest.

A few years ago, during my first meeting with a numbers-analytical, results-driven customer, the CEO-prospect said in response to my earliest questions, "We're not happy with being better than the average on customer complaints. I want zero complaints! Something's got to change, fast!" There's no doubt he was stressed, frustrated, and dissatisfied.

Asking questions can help analytical customers communicate their thoughts and feelings. Ask things like, "Why's this so important to you?" or "What are your biggest concerns about this project?" or "Do you have any reservations that give you pause about proceeding?"

Numbers Thinkers are reluctant risk-takers who usually have doubts or are cautious about a decision because they fear making wrong decisions. You can help them be forthcoming with questions about their concerns or fears.

GIVE THEM COMPELLING REASONS TO BUY BASED ON FACTS

It's not as common for Numbers Thinkers to make quick decisions as it is for Energetic Drivers. Then again, when presented with compelling, logical reasons to purchase, their sense of urgency is heightened, and a decision might happen fast. It happened to me in the 80s when I sold filtration services.

I asked a chemical engineer in charge of his company's large project, "Have you ever considered the merits of filtering the fluid before putting it down your wellbore?" He looked quizzingly at me and asked, "No, should I?" Since many engineers I sold to used analytical decision-making processes in their work, I knew the question was likely to create curiosity to know more.

"Yes," I said, "there are three reasons it could benefit you," and I explained my reasons. He then asked two more basic questions and surprised me by issuing a large purchase order. The sale was closed in under thirty minutes.

Your Numbers Thinker customer wants to be confident they're making an accurate decision. An approach that makes them comfortable because it aligns with how they like to buy, is one of the fastest ways to win their support.

COMMUNICATE IN THEIR LANGUAGE

George is the primary decision-maker for a boat manufacturer. His answers and questions showed he was a strong Numbers Thinker by being careful, detailed, and organized. His desk's neat stack of charts and graphs was a dead giveaway, too.

When we met, I took careful notes, logging the points he emphasized and those he didn't, as well as his desired outcomes and objectives. In addition to mentioning the referral that initially caused him to reach out, George had two issues: what return on investment could he expect, and what timeline would be required?

To answer a Numbers Thinker's questions, it's a good idea to remember how they like to process information. Analytical thinkers have a keen ability to break down complex problems into smaller, more manageable pieces. So, to speak their language, you should organize data in bullet points or outline form. They also appreciate the use of numbers and specifics like "There are three possibilities," "There are two main options," or "This approach will give you three benefits."

After our first meeting, I recapped George's goals and what he'd stressed with me. After I finished my outline, I asked, "Does it accurately capture what you want to accomplish?" He responded enthusiastically, "Yes, that's exactly what I want!"

Listening well and organizing communication helps your Numbers Thinker customer visually process and digest what you're trying to say accurately. When presented with a large amount of data or material, they become overwhelmed if it's not delivered effectively.

BE SELECTIVE WITH INFORMATION

You can avoid wasting the customer's time by looking for ways to offer information selectively.

Try asking, for example, questions like "Would it be helpful for you to know the three ways our service department can solve that problem and reduce your downtime?" Or, you can pause during a presentation and say, "I can keep going on this issue if you'd like, or we can switch to discuss something you'd prefer."

Another question I like to use with Numbers Thinkers is, "Did I answer your question completely, or is there something you'd like me to provide more information on?" The result is that you now guide and control the dialogue while appearing to give them control.

Let's return to George, whom I mentioned previously. By asking questions that engaged him in prioritizing the type of information he wanted, he was more committed to how my value would help him accomplish his objectives. I'm convinced it helped close the deal.

ANTICIPATE AND HANDLE THEIR SKEPTICISM DIRECTLY

Skepticism is hard-wired in Numbers Thinkers, so always be ready to deal with it. But skepticism can have many causes.

Ryan, a salesman for a specialty chemicals company and a Numbers Thinker himself, had trouble selling other styles when he encountered skepticism or any form of resistance. One of his biggest problems was that he mistook skepticism for a lack of trust, until I coached him through it.

In Ryan's situation, he had to realize that his customers were wary, not because they didn't trust him, but because they needed reassurance that he would stay committed and remain accessible to them after the sale.

This is an easy problem to fix. In Ryan's coaching, we laid out a couple of questions to ask regarding how they preferred him to remain accessible and then had him lay out a plan explaining how he could stay involved and ease their concerns. It paid off, too. One customer told Ryan it was the main deciding factor in awarding his company the sale.

SELL QUALITY, CAREFULLY

Sales presentation lines like "Our product is second to none" or "We have high-quality products" means nothing to the analytical buyer and will undoubtedly turn them off unless you have the convincing reasons to back it up.

There's a powerful formula for selling quality. It consists of five steps.

Step one: *Welcome a thorough discussion and critical analysis.* The customer will put your product's features under a microscope, and you want to encourage a complete examination. Set several meetings with product experts in your company if needed so they can also assess all possible advantages and downsides with your people.

Step two: *Address each issue honestly.* Emphasize that you want them to study the facts and reach their conclusions. They need to see that you're not trying to sell them something, but are truthfully looking after their needs.

Step three: *Call in help if necessary.* Be informed and very comfortable discussing the details that interest them. If you're not comfortable, call in the support you need. The worst mistake you can make is attempting to appear knowledgeable when you're not.

Step four: *Explain the steps included in your quality assurance process.* Clarify how these steps achieve high quality while mitigating the customer's risks. Reassure them that other customers in similar situations have used your solution and continue to use it because of its reliability. You want to gather sufficient explanation, supporting facts, or evidence that gives your buyer good reasons why they can feel confident about moving forward.

Step five: *Use verbiage that supports your case for quality.* Analytical customers are cautious, and using favorable terms will lessen their worries. For example, use words such as "safety and security," "consistency," "warranty," and ""guarantee," and also use descriptions like "proven," "dependable," or "reliable."

Many Numbers Thinkers go out of their way to be precise, finding a perfect solution to their needs. Right from the start of your sales meetings, they'll look to appease their cautious nature, and if you adapt to their style needs effectively, they'll like and trust you faster.

USE GOALS, TIMELINES, AND ACTION STEPS

One of my most memorable sales calls was with Andy, an executive sales leader of ten regional sales managers. Andy was an authoritarian, results-driven, direct character who challenged my points and recommendations and questioned my training investment ROI forecast. If he engaged my services, he insisted on a detailed training plan that outlined the objectives, performance criteria to measure effectiveness, and the implementation steps.

None of this bothered me because I could immediately relate with his Energetic Driver and Numbers Thinker tendencies. Knowing this helped me successfully move him through my sales process.

Providing Andy with a document where he could look at the training process, objectives, and criteria to assess ROI was precisely what he asked for. As soon as he read the document, he remarked, "Good, very good, this is perfect." It was surprising how quickly he approved my proposal, too.

Analytical customers like clear goals, timelines, and action steps. It makes them more comfortable with the decision, and with you.

WILL NOT STAND FOR BEING RUSHED

Numbers Thinkers believe in the axiom, "Don't rush things."

They'll resent it if you pressure them to decide faster than they're prepared to do. They need adequate time to analyze information and come up with questions.

For example, when asked a difficult question, an analytical person might take a few moments to formulate their thoughts before responding. Don't cut them off or talk over them when they speak. Keep silent and let them finish. The more freedom you create for free-flowing dialogue, the more they'll share.

Also, don't be alarmed if they're quiet for a while. Remember, they may be taking their time to run the numbers, get inside support, and be entirely comfortable with the decision. As a result, they might not get back to you as soon as you wish.

If you're uneasy, gently nudge them with questions such as, "Curious if your decision timeline has changed?" or "Checking to see if you thought of any additional info you'd like from me?" They will appreciate the considerate follow-up.

ASK THOUGHT-PROVOKING QUESTIONS

You'll win more deals if you get analytical-type decision-makers to see your company's value positively and to think differently about their needs. Recently, I coached a client who did what I'm talking about with excellent results.

Mick runs his family's second-generation commercial construction company. The company primarily works with investors and project managers who choose construction companies. Most of their decision-makers are Numbers Thinkers or Energetic Drivers who are detail-oriented, skeptical, and demand accuracy and results.

Mick wanted to win more projects at higher margins and significantly increase sales revenue. We worked twice monthly on asking better questions instead of automatically launching into his standard pitch that wasn't producing results. Immediately he noticed a positive change in prospects' responses, such as "I've never thought about that before" or "That's a good question no one's ever asked." When his approach changed, customer engagement and interest improved.

Within a year, Mick's small business closed significantly more jobs than the company had ever handled and at higher margins. Eventually, they won so many new contracts that they couldn't take all of them.

FIND THEIR RELUCTANCE AND RESOLVE IT

Nicholas, the National Strategic Account Manager for my client, a commercial building restoration service, faced much resistance when he attempted to expand the company's footprint. Prospective customers didn't know about his company and didn't want to use them because they were happy with their current provider.

All the pushback made the CEO consider scrapping the effort. Instead, he asked me to coach Nicholas on selling to executives and management, and then he would reevaluate.

Ultimately, Nicolas overcame the resistance and expanded into three new states. It was a massive success for Nicholas, and the CEO was ecstatic with the results. I'll tell you how he did it.

He devised a go-to-market value proposition, something he could explain in under thirty seconds that could be tailored to fit virtually any customer. He gathered internal performance numbers on customer satisfaction, repeat customers, and delivery data to sell his company's benefits and prove what they could do.

He created great discovery questions to uncover typical, unique, and unrecognized needs to which Nicholas could link his strengths and provide specific value. Besides that, he learned how to sell to executives with analytical, results-driven, and numbers-oriented style needs.

Ultimately, nothing will stop you from successfully landing appointments and winning new deals with Numbers Thinkers if you know how to adapt to their style preferences.

POSSIBLE QUESTIONS TO ASK

You'll want to use questions that encourage the customer to think deeply about what they need and why. They're most interested in facts and figures, so some of your questions should be tailored towards getting them to open up on the type of data they find useful in making an informed, accurate decision. Try asking questions like the following by changing them to fit your style and your customer's situation.

1. What challenges have you faced in the past when making decisions for x?
2. How do you prioritize price versus prioritizing quality with this purchase?
3. Have you considered the advantages of using x to cut your costs and increase x?
4. How regularly do you review your current supplier's product performance? (Or: What metrics does your current supplier use to ensure continuous performance?)
5. What specific metrics/measurables do you look at when evaluating new products or services? What kind of information from me would be most helpful to you in deciding?
6. Is there an ideal timeline for implementation you have in mind? What's the motivation for that timeline?
7. Could you tell me about any similar products or services that have been successful (or unsuccessful) in use throughout your organization?
8. Are there any specific features you consider essential? (What information would you like to have regarding our product's capabilities?)
9. How comfortable are you with taking some risk when investing in a new technology solution? What are your greatest fears taking these risks?
10. How are you going to measure the impact my product/service will make for your situation?

TOP 10 CHAPTER HIGHLIGHTS

1. Skip the "How great we are" speech and don't use a pitchy presentation.
2. Build credibility and receptivity by openly evaluating all sides to an issue.
3. Be more formal, less casual, and skip the small talk unless they start it.
4. Ask pertinent questions to prepare detailed information they'll find useful.
5. Don't assume value (the curse of knowledge), link value to their drivers.
6. Provide goals, action steps, and timelines.
7. Do your homework; run the numbers, quantify.
8. Follow through on all requests for studies, results, data, testimonials.
9. Answer their questions or skepticism directly, don't dismiss or be evasive.
10. Ask thought-provoking questions and listen with comprehension.

CONCLUSION:
PUTTING IT TO USE

At the start of *Selling to ELON*, we read an inspiring story about an insurance agent who transformed his career into the CEO of multiple agencies. His account is a testament to the value of comprehending and adapting to the unique personalities we encounter in life.

By understanding ourselves and recognizing the style preferences of the Energetic Driver, Likable Communicator, Obliging Helper, and Numbers Thinker, we can understand our customers better and leverage our strengths while working on our shortcomings. Equipped with this skill, it becomes possible to quickly build credibility and earn trust and rapport with customers on a deeper level, enabling us to close new deals and win hearts and minds.

In *Selling to ELON*, we have explored numerous insights and lessons to help adapt our messages to match individual personality style preferences. To use these strategies successfully, frequently review the principles and steps until they become second nature as you build lasting relationships with customers and coworkers.

Your future presents limitless opportunities for personal and professional growth as you apply these practical yet powerful methods to your daily life. Here is a summary of what you've read.

ENERGETIC DRIVER

ENERGETIC DRIVER'S STRENGTHS AS A SALESPERSON:
Determined, competitive, results-oriented, embraces challenges, handles rejection, and initiates action.

HOW TO SPOT AN ENERGETIC DRIVER IN 4 MINUTES:
- Greets with formality, direct eye contact, a firm handshake.
- Outspoken, to the point, opinionated, assertive.
- Decisive, fast-paced.
- Might direct the discussion, interrupt, correct, or challenge.
- Bottom line, results-driven, focused on tasks not people.
- Risk taker if better, faster results are possible.
- Email/texting: direct, straightforward with little explanation, to the point, uses assertive words or tone, may be forceful or demanding, focused on results and goals.

WHEN SELLING TO ENERGETIC DRIVER CUSTOMERS:
- Be direct, avoid small talk.
- Come organized, present ideas in a logical flow.
- Focus on results, provide sufficient options.
- Don't do "information avalanches."
- If you disagree, differ with facts not the person.
- Tailor-fit solutions to fit specific problems.
- Answer questions or objections directly.
- Be an excellent listener; intense attentiveness.

THE COMMUNICATION STYLE OF ENERGETIC DRIVERS:
When it comes to small talk, Energetic Drivers often take charge of conversations and steer them in their desired direction. They ask quick questions or expect rapid responses from others. They prefer shorter conversations rather than long-winded ones and might become impatient if conversations linger too long.

Instead of subtlety, they express themselves with certainty. They may use blunt and frank language, preferring honesty and clarity over politeness and ambiguity. Rather than ramble on hesitantly, they'll explain themselves confidently and in complete sentences.

Interaction-wise, Energetic Drivers may come across as intimidating due to their high energy, decisiveness, and strong presence. Even so, once they see your competence and confidence as a sales professional, asking open-ended questions will stimulate sufficient conversation.

QUESTIONS TO ASK:
1. What are your main goals and how would you potentially like us to help you accomplish them?
2. What's your timeline for this project, and how critical is it that the solution is implemented by then?
3. Which key performance indicators are most significant?
4. What are your most pressing challenges, and what are the consequences if they aren't solved adequately? How can we solve them for you?
5. How do you measure ROI when it comes to purchasing products/services?
6. What kind of priority does this project have for you? Your company?

LIKABLE COMMUNICATOR

LIKABLE COMMUNICATOR'S STRENGTHS AS A SALESPERSON:
Pleasant, outgoing, conversational, energetic, upbeat, articulate, persuasive, and optimistic.

HOW TO SPOT A LIKABLE COMMUNICATOR IN 4 MINUTES:
- Greets people eagerly, welcoming, may engage in light banter or small talk.

- Uses open gestures, active facial expressions, expressive body language.
- Talkative, may stray from the purpose of the communication, lose track of time.
- May lean forward or close physical distance.
- Action-based, faster pace desired.
- Optimistic, enthusiastic attitude, positive approach to things.
- Email/texting: wordy, colorful, lively language and may inject humor or personality, uses exclamation points or emoticons to express emotion.

WHEN SELLING TO LIKABLE COMMUNICATORS:
- Develop credibility, trust, and rapport early.
- Limit the details; get to the point.
- Let them talk, redirect with questions.
- Show outward enthusiasm for your product or service.
- Develop rapport; let them to get to know you.
- Provide impressive testimonials and case studies.
- Be an excellent listener; verbally/non-verbally responsive.

THE COMMUNICATION STYLE OF LIKABLE COMMUNICATORS:
Likable Communicators are talkative, may tell stories, and their tone often changes when they get excited. They are usually confident and comfortable speaking their minds and will do so quickly and spontaneously.

During small talk, a Likable Communicator is adept at interacting with others because they're friendly and outgoing. They like to be the center of attention and tend to appear self-assured.

While they might ramble on for a while without stopping to think about the time or whether or not they're on the topic, you can easily redirect them with a guided question.

QUESTIONS TO ASK:
1. What are your goals or vision for this project?
2. How does the problem or opportunity impact operations, employees, or customers?
3. What solutions are you personally leaning toward? Why?
4. In addition to price, what are the main criteria/factors driving your decision? (Get specifics.)
5. Based on what you've seen so far, how comfortable (or confident) are you that our product will help you achieve your goals?
6. How are you going to measure the impact my product/service will make for your situation?

OBLGING HELPER

OBLGING HELPER'S STRENGTHS AS A SALESPERSON:
Amiable, patient, low-key, is steady and methodical, a good team player and listener, and hides emotions well.

HOW TO SPOT AN OBLIGING HELPER IN 4 MINUTES:
- Greets people in a warm, cheerful manner, smiles.
- Will be accommodating, supportive, and avoids challenging others.
- Has a leisurely, easygoing pace.
- Soft-spoken, listens patiently.
- Relationship-oriented, welcomes interaction.
- Cautious, requires ample time to commit, prefers minimal risk or change.
- Email/texting: courteous tone, expresses support, helpfulness, or appreciation, can be detailed and thorough with facts and examples, often end as they begin with kind words.

WHEN SELLING TO OBLIGING HELPERS:

- Use a relaxed, easy approach to talk through their goals and needs.
- Try to engage in brief small talk before launching into business.
- Stress guarantees, testimonials to reinforce that their decision is right.
- Support them involving others in the decision.
- Make your value clear, quantify the positive differences.
- Don't pressure them to decide quickly; get small commitments leading up to a purchase.
- Introduce them to service staff, technical experts, managers, etc.
- Be an excellent listener, use verbal/nonverbal responsiveness.

THE COMMUNICATION STYLE OF OBLIGING HELPERS:

They tend to interact with a smile, make good eye contact, and engage in small talk before getting down to business. They listen carefully and intently.

Slow and steady is how Obliging Helpers like to communicate verbally, which may come across as being indecisive or unsure of themselves. They may not always speak up when they disagree because their motivation is harmony and approval, so it's essential to ask for their opinion and test their commitment with questions.

Obliging Helpers may seem low-key in communication, but they have solid viewpoints and good ideas that you'll need to uncover by asking engaging questions.

QUESTIONS TO ASK:

1. What are your top priorities or goals when it comes to this purchase?
2. Do you have any concerns or reservations about my solution? Are there any other factors we haven't discussed that will influence your decision?

3. Are you loyal to any existing supplier relationships or partnerships for this purchase?
4. Are you involving the input of others in the decision? Is there a particular way I can help you help others understand my product and its value?
5. Do you know of anyone on your purchasing team who does not favor purchasing my product? How would you suggest that I work with them?
6. How are you going to measure the impact my product/service will make for your situation?

THE NUMBERS THINKER

NUMBERS THINKERS' STRENGTHS AS SALESPEOPLE:
Analytical, detailed, and thorough, does quality work, follows procedures or systems, is accurate and precise with very high standards.

HOW TO SPOT AN NUMBERS THINKER IN 4 MINUTES:
- Greets you matter-of-factly, formally.
- Uses few to no gestures, avoids facial expressions, rests hand on chin.
- Slow and deliberate speaking pace.
- To the point, direct.
- Questions information, opinions, or conclusions to increase understanding.
- Values facts and figures, scrutinizes the details, information-driven.
- Good listening attentiveness and comprehension; writes things down.
- Email/texting: is organized, precise, and detailed, uses facts and evidence with logical views, may be technical, offer solutions or instructions, focused on results, uses little emotion or pleasantries.

WHEN SELLING NUMBERS THINKERS:

- Prepare detailed, well-researched information.
- Don't assume the product's value is obvious (the curse of knowledge).
- Be more formal/professional and less casual.
- Provide a timeline, action steps and deadlines.
- Do your homework; run the numbers and quantify the product's value.
- Promptly follow through on requests for studies, data, or testimonials.
- Answer their questions directly, don't dismiss or be iffy.
- Be an excellent listener and ask *thinkers'* questions.

THE COMMUNICATION STYLE OF NUMBERS THINKERS:

Numbers Thinkers are known for being specific in their choice of words and numbers and avoid generalizations and slang.

They're not fond of small talk. Numbers Thinkers prefer to get straight to the point and have an important conversation. They can feel uncomfortable when asked to express themselves beyond basic facts and will quickly change body postures, becoming more closed or distant if a question puts them on the spot.

Numbers Thinkers tend to avoid eye contact that lasts too long. When they do respond, they're unhurried and careful, which can come across as being dodgy or hesitant but it's really due to their thoughtful approach to communication.

Numbers Thinkers like the details but can miss the big-picture points you present, so posing follow-up questions is essential.

QUESTIONS TO ASK:

1. How do you prioritize price versus quality with this purchase?
2. Have you considered the advantages of using x to cut your costs and increase x?

3. What specific metrics/measurables do you look at when evaluating new products or services? What kind of information from me would be most helpful to you in deciding?
4. Are there any specific features you consider essential? (What information would you like to have regarding our product's capabilities?)
5. How comfortable are you with taking some risk when investing in a new technology solution? What are your greatest fears taking these risks?
6. Which of my product's benefits are most appealing to you at this point?

⚡ RESOURCES AND LEARNING

E.L.O.N. STYLES ASSESSMENTS: www.elonstyles.com

The E.L.O.N. Styles assessment, provided in partnership with CraftMetrics International, is a widely-trusted personal development and hiring tool which assesses individual preferences and behaviors. With over 1 million individuals taking the CraftMetrics assessments, the accuracy and effectiveness of the E.L.O.N. assessment results have been extensively validated by numerous studies conducted by psychologists and researchers.

The E.L.O.N. Styles reports provide valuable insights to understand yourself and others accurately. They enable you to tailor your approach to others' communication styles to build instant rapport, establish trust, and sell your ideas or products with outstanding results.

Mark has been a licensed and certified partner for over 20 years with CraftMetrics. You can work directly with Mark for a personal review of your E.L.O.N. Styles report or your training needs.

Visit www.salesrevenuecoach.com to learn more, or call:
+1 (417) 883-7434 to start the discussion.

ABOUT THE AUTHOR

MARK HOLMES is a consultant and speaker/coach on increasing sales, service, and employee performance whose client list reads like a veritable Who's Who in commerce—from international oilfield services in the UK and biopharmaceutical manufacturing in the USA to iconic brands like Dunkin', Bass Pro Shops, Cisco and Chick-fil-A.

He frequently speaks on performance, sales, and service, and his insights have been featured in the *Wall Street Journal*, *FOX Business*, *Sales & Marketing Management*, and the *Chicago Tribune*. In addition to his consulting company, Mark has owned a radio station and a fitness center in the Ozarks area of Missouri, where he lives with his wife and family.